FUNCTIONAL SKILLS:

ENGLISH LEVEL 1

Roslyn Whitley Willis

Published by
Lexden Publishing Ltd
www.lexden-publishing.co.uk

About the Author

Roslyn Whitley Willis has worked as a Key Skills tutor, assessor, verifier and co-ordinator in further and higher education. Additionally she has worked independently as a Key Skills consultant. She is the author of 16 widely accepted Key Skills text books.

Roslyn has incorporated, and extended, the principles that were successful in her Key Skills text books which she sees as key to helping centres make the transition from Key Skills to Functional Skills and assisting students to gain the qualification.

To ensure that your book is up to date visit:
www.lexden-publishing.co.uk/functionalskills/update.htm

Acknowledgements

A special mention to my good friend Diana Outhwaite who provided me with some ideas to include in the Brush Up your Writing and Speaking Skills.
– *Roslyn Whitley Willis.*

First Published in 2009 by Lexden Publishing Ltd.

British Library Cataloguing in Publication Data.

A CIP record of this book is available from the British Library

ISBN 978-1-904995-47-0

Typeset and designed by Lexden Publishing Ltd.

Printed by Lightning Source.

Lexden Publishing Ltd
Email: info@lexden-publishing.co.uk
www.lexden-publishing.co.uk

CONTENTS

FUNCTIONAL SKILLS: ENGLISH LEVEL 1

INTRODUCTION

The purpose of Functional Skills English is to provide a qualification that will prepare you, the learner, for the skills you will need in work, for progressing through education and in your everyday life.

Having these skills will help the individual person and the employee to work confidently, effectively and independently.

The skills which are important include being able to:

- read and understand information of various types, such as instructions; timetables; advertisements; tables; graphs; letters from organisations; newspaper articles; maps; and information located in a range of books and the world wide web;

- show you understand the documents you read by identifying if they express an opinion or facts and putting that information into your own words;

- write a variety of documents, expressing yourself clearly and using your own words;

- write documents that are laid out correctly and include all the relevant details;

- write documents that present ideas and facts in a logical order;

- write a range of documents such as those required in business – letters, memos and emails – and those needed in personal life-like letters and instructions;

- write documents that are suited to the reader and the subject;

- write documents that are formal (such as a business letter or a memo), or informal (such as a fax or email or a personal letter to a friend);

- write documents that convey the information and your meaning clearly, and that use correct English grammar and punctuation and spelling;

- listen in group and one-to-one discussions and show an understanding of what is being said by others;

- speak in groups, and to individuals, to exchange ideas and opinions and express your ideas clearly so the listeners can follow what you say.

The material in this book gives you the opportunity to acquire, and apply, this knowledge and these skills.

This book is in three sections:

Section 1 gives guidance on some aspects of English grammar to help your writing skills, and some guidance on words to avoid when involved in discussions.

Section 2 provides Reference sheets which cover the background information to prepare you for the activities that follow. These Reference Sheets aid your learning and understanding, they can also be used for revision.

Section 3 is made up of practice tasks covering a range of employment sectors. These tasks are designed to help you produce work at the correct level and also help you become confident and competent when you take the assessment of Functional English Level 1. The assessment will test your ability to apply what you have learnt in the subject to everyday contexts which are not linked to specific employment sectors.

SECTION 1

BRUSH UP YOUR WRITING AND SPEAKING SKILLS

Apostrophes

Using apostrophes correctly is easy. Just follow these rules.

The two main reasons for using apostrophes are:

1   to show a letter, or letters, are omitted in a word; and

2   to show possession.

Rule 1 — to show where a letter (or letters) has been missed out

don't	means	do not	the apostrophe is placed where the letter "o" has been left out.
I don't (do n[o]t) know where the hotel is located.			

didn't	means	did not	the apostrophe is placed where the letter "o" has been left out.
I didn't (did n[o]t) go to college yesterday.			

I'm	means	I am	the apostrophe is placed where the letter "a" has been left out.
I'm (I [a]m) going to the party on Saturday.			
I do not feel as if I'm (I [a]m) able to visit him.			

she'll	means	she will	the apostrophe is placed where the letters "w" and "i" have been left out.
She'll (she [wi]ll) come to the wedding next month.			

haven't	means	have not	the apostrophe is placed where the letter "o" has been left out.
I haven't (have n[o]t) got an examination date yet.			

| it's | means | it is | the apostrophe is placed where the letter "i" has been left out. |

It's (it [i]s) easy to get to her home.

It's (it [i]s) not difficult to pass the test.

| we're | means | we are | the apostrophe is placed where the letter "a" has been left out. |

We're (we [a]re) all going to the fair in February.

I am not sure we're (we [a]re) entered for the examination.

| they'll | means | they will | the apostrophe is placed where the letters "w" and "i" have been left out. |

They'll (they [wi]ll) decide whether to live in Australia.

| who's | means | who is | the apostrophe is placed where the letter "i" has been left out. |

Who's (who [i]s) the best driver?

| you're | means | you are | the apostrophe is placed where the letter "a" has been left out. |

You're (you [a]re) not taking this seriously.

I am not sure you're (you [a]re) going to pass.

Exercise

Try to put the correct word using the apostrophe in the following sentences. (**Be careful! There are some which are not in the previous examples, so you will have to think about them!**)

1   (We are) _____ bringing father home from hospital next

Monday.

2   (It is) _____ so easy to do this exercise.

3   (They are) _____ going to Budapest for their holiday this year.

4   It (is not) _____ his car which was stolen.

5   He is not sure (I am) _____ invited to the fair.

6   (It is) _____ easy for you to say that, but I (have not)

_____ got a clue.

7   (What is) _____ the matter with your car, Harry?

8   (It is) _____ the exhaust, and (they are) _____ not

sure they can put it right.

9   (You are) _____ going to have to hire a car (are not) _____

you?

10   Yes, (it will) _____ be an expensive few days when (I have)

_____ not got my car.

Rule 2 — To show someone, or something, possesses (owns) something

Singular Words

In the English language we do not say things like ....

collar of the cat	(singular — one cat)
hat of the boy	(singular — one boy)
shoes of the lady	(singular — one lady)
legs of the chair	(singular — one chair)
house of the mother	(singular — one mother)

Instead we structure sentences which indicate someone, or something, possesses (owns) something by using an apostrophe.

The order of the words in the sentences that require apostrophes is this:

1st	**2nd**
who or **what** does the owning	**what** is owned

For example:

In the phrase '**collar of the cat**' ask yourself — **who owns what**?

Answer: one cat owns the collar.

So the order is '**cat**' then '**collar**'.

In the phrase '**house of the mother**' ask yourself — **who owns what**?

Answer: one mother owns the house.

So the order is '**mother**' then '**house**'.

Where do I put in the Apostrophe?

!!!! Don't worry — It's easy !!!!

Follow these five simple steps

Step 1:   write down the word which represents the person or thing doing the owning.

cat

Step 2:   next to that write what is owned.

cat **collar**

Step 3:   think once more about who or what does the owning, in this case **cat**, and underline it.

<u>cat</u> collar

Step 4:   next put the apostrophe **after** the <u>underlined</u> word.

<u>cat</u>' collar

Step 5:   finally, as the word **cat** is singular, add a letter **s** <u>after</u> the apostrophe.

<u>cat</u>'s collar

Let's try it with "house of the mother".

Step 1:   write down the word which represents the person or thing doing the owning.

mother

Step 2:   next write what is owned.

mother **house**

Step 3:   think once more about who or what does the owning, in this case **mother**, and underline it.

<u>mother</u> house

Step 4:   next put the apostrophe **after** the <u>underlined</u> word.

<u>mother</u>' house

Step 5:   finally, as the word **mother** is singular, add a letter **s** after the apostrophe.

<u>mother</u>'s house

Let's try it with "shoes of the lady".

Step 1:   write down the word which represents the person or thing doing the owning.

lady

Step 2:   next write what is owned.

lady **shoes**

Step 3:   think once more about who or what does the owning, in this case **lady**, and <u>underline</u> it.

<u>lady</u> shoes

Step 4:   next put the apostrophe **after** the <u>underlined</u> word.

<u>lady</u>' shoes

Step 5:   finally, as the word **lady** is singular, add a letter **s** after the apostrophe.

<u>lady</u>'s shoes

To Summarise

1   Write down the word representing who or what does the owning.

2   Write down the word of what is owned.

3   Underline the word representing who or what does the owning.

4   Put the apostrophe **after** the underlined word.

5   If the word is **singular** add an 's' **after** the apostrophe.

Exercise

Put in the apostrophe for each of the following, singular, owners:

1   the boy owning the hat _____

2   the chair owning the legs _____

3   the man owning the briefcase _____

4   the dog owning the bone _____

5   the student owning the pen _____

Rule 2 – To show a group of people, or things, possess (own) something

Plural words (ending in the letter s)

Examples:

ladies owning club	(many ladies)
boys owning football	(many boys)
dogs owning collars	(many dogs)

In the phrase **'ladies owning club'** ask yourself **who owns what?**

Answer: the ladies (plural) own a club.

So the order is **'ladies'** then **'club'**.

Where do I put in the apostrophe?

!!!! Good news – there are only four steps in this one !!!

Step 1: write down the word that represents the people or things doing the owning.

ladies

Step 2: next write what is owned.

ladies club (many ladies owning a club)

Step 3: think once more about who or what does the owning, in this case **ladies**, and <u>underline</u> it.

<u>ladies</u> club

Step 4: **finally** put the apostrophe **after** the <u>underlined</u> word.

<u>ladies</u>' club

There's no need to put a letter **s** after the word <u>ladies</u> as it ends in a letter **s**.

Let's try it with boys owning a football.

Step 1: write down the word that represents the people or things doing the owning.

boys

Step 2: next write what is owned.

boys football (one football owned by many boys)

Step 3: think once more about who or what does the owning, in this case **boys**, and <u>underline</u> it.

<u>boys</u> football

Step 4: **finally** put the apostrophe **after** the <u>underlined</u> word.

<u>boys</u>' football

There's no need to put a letter **s** after the word <u>boys</u> as it ends in a letter **s**.

Let's try it with dogs owning collars.

Step 1:   write down the word which represents the people or things doing the owning.

dogs

Step 2:   next write what is owned.

dogs **collars** (many dogs owning many collars)

Step 3:   think once more about who or what does the owning, in this case **dogs**, and underline it.

<u>**dogs**</u> collars

Step 4:   **finally** put the apostrophe **after** the <u>underlined</u> word.

<u>**dogs**</u>' collars

There's no need to put a letter **s** after the word <u>dogs</u> as it ends in a letter **s**.

NOTE: There's no need to put an apostrophe in collars because it's just a plural word – it doesn't own anything and there's no letter omitted.

To Summarise

1   Write down the word representing who or what does the owning.

2   Write down the word of what is owned.

3   Underline the word representing who or what does the owning.

4   Put the apostrophe **after** the underlined word.

Exercise

Put in the apostrophe for each of the following, plural, owners.

Remember: it's only the people or things doing the owning that need an apostrophe.

1   the clubs owning the football ground _____

2   the students owning the text books _____

3   the tutors owning the pens _____

4   the cars owning the exhausts _____

5   the boxers owning competitions _____

One Extra Rule About Apostrophes

You have learnt that whatever or whoever does the owning has the apostrophe somewhere.

You know how to work out that "somewhere" – write the word down, underline it, then put the apostrophe **after** the word.

So you have: man's son; ladies' meeting; students' calculator; dogs' bones

But

When the thing/person that owns is already plural — children, men, women - then you must put the apostrophe after that word, as usual, **then put on the letter 's'.**

For example: the <u>men</u>'s club   (one club owned by many men)

               the <u>children</u>'s toys   (many children owning many toys)

               the <u>women</u>'s clothes   (the clothes owned by many women).

You are still thinking about who or what does the owning, putting the apostrophe after it, then adding an s.

There's an exception, but don't worry about it.

You will have possibly seen a reference to a Charles Dickens's book, or Tom Jones's singing career? My name is Willis, so you would be quite correct in writing "Roslyn

Willis's book". This is not wrong, but this does look messy and therefore it's quite acceptable when names end in the letter **s** to just put the apostrophe after the **s**. It's so much nicer to read Roslyn Willis' book, and Tom Jones' voice.

So, when the word ends in s put the apostrophe after it and STOP.

Exercise

Put in the apostrophe for each of the following. Think carefully about the word that represents who, or what, is doing the owning, and if it is plural or singular.

1   The cat owning a toy _____

2   The school owning the trophy _____

3   The piano owning the keys _____

4   The cats owning the whiskers _____

5   The gentlemen owning a club _____

6   The policemen owning uniforms _____

7   The student owning a book _____

8   The woman owning an umbrella _____

9   The car owning a steering wheel _____

10   The man owning a briefcase _____

I Before E — Except After C

Sometimes it is necessary to learn some spelling rules to help you get your work correct. The "i" before "e" rule is one of them.

It's an easy general rule: **use i before e, except after c** (when the sound is "ee").

Which means that you will **usually** use **ie** in such words as:

believe; sieve; grieve.

But you will use **ei** when the **e** follows the letter **c** in such words as:

receive; receipt; perceive.

Of course, there are always exceptions such as **weird**, **weight**, **protein**, **vacancies** and **caffeine**, but that's all the more reason to use your dictionary.

Exercise

Choose the word that is spelt correctly in each of the following sentences. **Then find each word in the grid in the next exercise.**

1   I must achieve/acheive better examination results this year.

2   It is easy to believe/beleive he is the best student.

3   The ceiling/cieling of our kitchen needs to be painted.

4   A train that carries goods, not passengers, is called a frieght/freight train.

5   We get on very well with our neighbours/nieghbours.

6   I offered her a peice/piece of cake but she refused it.

7   Our local priest/preist is retiring next year.

8   When you buy goods you should always keep the receipt/reciept in case you need to return the goods to the shop.

9   Queen Victoria is said to have had the longest reign/riegn in the United Kingdom.

10   It was a releif/relief to see him looking so well after his operation.

11   At Christmas it is common to hear the sleigh/sliegh bells in the clear, quiet night.

12   I donated blood the other day. It involved putting a needle into my veins/viens.

13   Please weigh/wiegh the butter carefully. If you get it wrong, the cake will be ruined.

14   This year the farmers say their crops have a greater yeild/yield than last year.

Now use your answers to find the words in the word search in the next exercise.

Exercise

Now find the words you found in the previous exercise in this word search.

```
M A L M H E O S D F G Q O R A
U K O Z F P B T N W L X D C E
R E L I E F H G I E W D H G V
U T E P V I M O N E T I N H E
S R U O B H G I E N E I G V I
T P R T Z S B A A V L I S V L
X S I H P I S J E I E T E D E
S L E E D I X V E L H I L G B
L C H I C E E C S G N E L E A
L J I X R E Y C I S I U R G W
A C Z C Q P Q E E Y M J J X N
C E Y M D L R E S R Z V S K D
U V I U V F U N G I E R H R X
S I F T D Q X X D H Z T M U H
V J Z L K U K E I C S Z A R F
```

"There", "Their" and "They're"

There wedding is in August. Their very keen to have all the arrangements go well. They're cousins will be travelling all the way from New Zealand so there very happy. Everyone their should have a very happy day.

Can you spot the words which are used incorrectly in the above sentences?

No? It all looks right?

These words look and sound similar and sometimes it can be difficult to decide how to use *there*, *their* and *they're* correctly.

Read the information in each of the examples, test yourself, then go back to those sentences and you should be able to correct them with ease.

There

This indicates a location, so when you use this word you might be talking about a direction.

> **Examples using "there":**
>
> **There** are the crayons I thought I had lost.
>
> My house is over **there**.
>
> **Tip** It is a place word so it has the word **here** in it. (*See page 24.*)

Their

This word indicates that more than one person, or thing, possesses something.

> **Examples using "their":**
>
> Ask them if they want to book **their** holiday yet.
>
> It is always easy to see **their** point of view.
>
> **Tip:** As this word can relate to people think "her" and "him" (e and i) — their.

They're

Because this word has an apostrophe in it, it is an indication that something has been left out. In this case it is the letter "a". (*See "Apostrophes" on page 4.*)

This word means they (a)re.

Examples using "they're":

> **They're** going to buy a new car next year.

> I cannot contact Paul and Roisin as **they're** out of the office today.

Exercise

Try to put the correct "their", "there" or "they're" in the following sentences:

1   I have _____ examination results.

2   Sometimes _____ is no money in the cash dispenser at the bank.

3   It might be possible to get _____ by bus rather than by train.

4   The firm decided _____ should be some rules about flexitime hours.

5   _____ going to _____ cousin's wedding next week. Will it be possible for you to go _____?

6   It seems that _____ having a good time in Italy.

7   _____ always late, no matter what time we arrange.

8   _____ train is due into Bristol Temple Meads at 17:00.

9   _____ are quite a few people going to _____ party on Wednesday.

10   _____ always at the football match on Saturday, supporting _____ favourite team.

Now go back to the sentences at the top of *page 17* and find the errors. It should be easy now.

"To", "Two" and "Too"

My family is thinking of going two Barcelona for a long weekend too see a concert. We are trying two book to tickets with a low-cost airline, but this is proving too be difficult. Perhaps we will have two book with a more expensive airline.

Can you spot the words which are used incorrectly in the above sentences?

No? It all looks right?

These words look similar and they all sound the same so sometimes it can be difficult to decide how to use *to*, *two* and *too* correctly.

Read the information for each of the examples, test yourself, then go back to those sentences and you should be able to correct them with ease.

To

This is known as a **preposition** and is a word that indicates direction. A preposition is a word which is used to join words and create phrases, usually related to time or place.

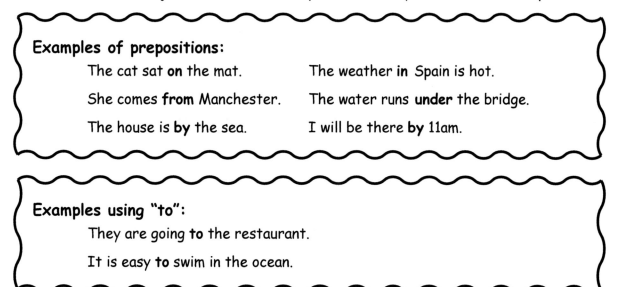

Examples of prepositions:

The cat sat **on** the mat.   The weather **in** Spain is hot.

She comes **from** Manchester.   The water runs **under** the bridge.

The house is **by** the sea.   I will be there **by** 11am.

Examples using "to":

They are going **to** the restaurant.

It is easy **to** swim in the ocean.

Two

Two is the written form of the number "2".

Examples using "two":

> The recipe uses **two** ounces of flour.
>
> There are **two** hundred bulbs in the garden.

Too

Too means "also" , "as well" and "very".

Examples using "too":

> Harriet said she was hungry, then Flavia said she was hungry **too** (also/as well).
>
> Niall wanted an ice-cream **too** (also/as well).
>
> His car is just too (very) big.
>
> The children's behaviour was **too** (very) mischievous.

Exercise

Try to put the correct "to", "too" or "two" in the following sentences:

1   He prefers _____ drive at night when there is not so much traffic
       on the road.

2   He set out _____ early for the shop _____ be open.

3   There are _____ days _____ go before we set off for Alicante.

4   I cannot go _____ the library until _____ o'clock. Is that
       _____ late?

5   It's always difficult _____ think about saving, but the _____ of
       us need to save for our holiday next year.

6   We have had _____ many problems with that company and certainly
       will not buy from them again.

7   Can you suggest any ways in which _____ solve these problems?

8   Jamie does not want _____ many guests at his wedding as it is going
       _____ be _____ expensive.

Now go back to the sentences at the top of *page 19* and find the errors. It
should be easy now.

"Where", "Were" and "We're"

Where going to Suzanna's wedding next week. We know you are going too. Were shall we meet you? Where going to travel on the M1 as far as Junction 28 so were able to make the short detour to your house if you want us to give you a lift to the wedding.

Can you spot the words which are used incorrectly in the above sentences?

No? It all looks right?

Because these words look similar it can be difficult to decide how to use *where*, *were* and *we're* correctly.

Read the information in each of the examples, test yourself, then go back to those sentences and you should be able to correct them with ease.

Where

This indicates a location.

Examples using "where":

> Where are they going for their holiday this year?

> I do not know where I am going.

Tip: Where is a place word so it has the word **here** in it. (*See page 24.*)

Were

This word indicates something happened in the past.

Examples using "were":

> They were almost home when the car broke down.

> We were going to Haslam's Mini Mart, but someone said it was closed.

We're

This word means we (a)re.

Because this word has an apostrophe in it, it is an indication that something has been left out. In this case it is the letter "a". (See "Apostrophes" on page 4.)

Examples using "we're":

> We're going to Harrogate to do some shopping.

> Tell us if we're not welcome.

Exercise

Try to put the correct "word", "where", "were" or "we're" in the following sentences:

1   _____ in the town is the new building going to be?

2   _____ they going to the cinema with you on Tuesday?

3   _____ in the town is the library?

4   I told him yesterday that _____ going skiing in January.

5   Do you think he's forgotten _____ we live?

6   _____ you able to hear the speaker from _____ you _____ at the back of the room?

7   Erinna is going to Malta and _____ going on holiday to Sicily next April.

8   Do you know _____ the nearest car park is situated?

9   Uncle Harry's advice is good. _____ going to have to save a lot of money if _____ going to be able to buy our first home next year.

10   _____ did she telephone from, do you know?

Now go back to the sentences at the top of *page 22* and find the errors. It should be easy now.

"Here", "Hear" or "Heard"?

"Hear you are Solomon. I herd you asking if the magazine was here", said Chris. "I here you are going to get hear by noon. Tell me if I herd correctly", said Issac.

Can you spot the words which are used incorrectly in the above sentences?

No? They look all right?

These words look and sound fairly similar so sometimes it can be difficult to decide how to use *here*, *hear* and *heard* correctly.

Read the information in each of the examples, test yourself, then go back to those sentences and you should be able to correct them with ease.

Here

This word usually relates to a place: **in** a place or **at** a place.

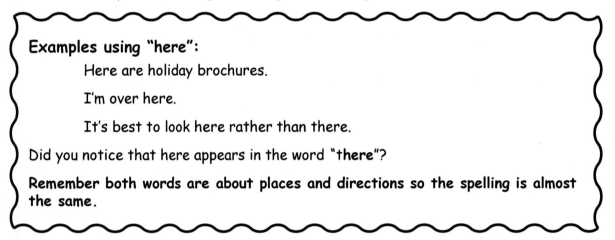

Examples using "here":

> Here are holiday brochures.
>
> I'm over here.
>
> It's best to look here rather than there.

Did you notice that here appears in the word "**there**"?

Remember both words are about places and directions so the spelling is almost the same.

Hear and Heard

Hear is used when talking about the present and the future, for example: "I hear you", "We will go to the meeting tomorrow to hear what they have to say".

Compare this with "heard" which is used to talk about the past. For example, "I heard you". "Yesterday I heard the new album by Nellie Furtado."

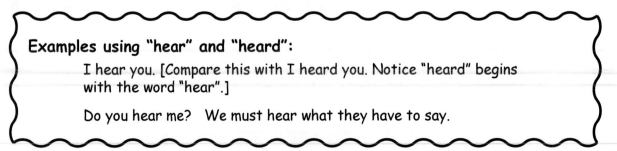

Examples using "hear" and "heard":

> I hear you. [Compare this with I heard you. Notice "heard" begins with the word "hear".]
>
> Do you hear me? We must hear what they have to say.

But What About "Herd"?

This sounds the same as the verb "heard", but it is a word used quite differently!

I'm sure you've heard about a herd of cows!

Remember: if it is anything to do with hearing "ear" appears in the word.

Exercise

Try to put the correct word, "here", "hear" or "heard" in the following sentences:

1 The valley was so quiet it was possible to _____ the skylark singing.

2 The cat's over _____, hiding in the corner.

3 I don't think they know their way _____.

4 Did I _____ you correctly?

5 It was only last week I _____ they were coming _____ for Christmas.

6 If they _____ the news about the hospital, why didn't they tell you?

7 At some point they will have to come _____, but we've _____ they are reluctant to do so.

8 In order for me to _____ you, you will have to come _____.

9 Perhaps you should leave them _____ whilst you go shopping.

10 Coming _____ was not the best thing to do. Have you _____ anything from them?

Now go back to the sentences at the top of *page 24* and find the errors. It should be easy now.

Do I Use "Amount" or "Number"?

These two words both refer to quantities, but are used differently according to the **noun** in the sentence. A noun is a word which usually refers to a place or a thing.

Examples of nouns:

The **cat** slept on the **sofa**.

An **egg** should be boiled in a **pan** for four minutes.

The **boy** always comes home with **mud** on his **shoes**.

Amount

Amount is used with singular nouns.

Examples:

(in each case the singular noun is emboldened)

The amount of **money** we have to spend each week is decreasing.

I only have a limited amount of **time** I can spend with you today.

You will have to give a certain amount of **thought** to this question.

Number

Number is used with **plural** nouns.

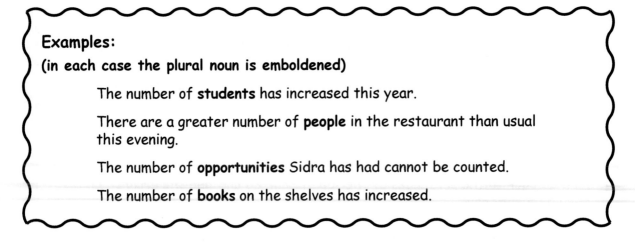

Examples:

(in each case the plural noun is emboldened)

The number of **students** has increased this year.

There are a greater number of **people** in the restaurant than usual this evening.

The number of **opportunities** Sidra has had cannot be counted.

The number of **books** on the shelves has increased.

Exercise

Try to put the correct word, "amount" or "number", in the following sentences.

In the first three sentences the **noun** is emboldened to help you.

TIP: Think what "amount" or "number" is describing (look for the noun). If it's singular use *amount*, if it's plural use *number*.

1   The _____ of holiday **destinations** in the brochure means we have plenty of choice.

2   There are a _____ of **jobs** to be done before we can go home today.

3   I was shocked by the _____ of **help** Petri needed with his project.

4   The _____ of clothes in her wardrobe is quite impressive.

5   I only have a small _____ of money to spend on presents for my family.

6   I have to write a project containing a large _____ of pages.

7   You will need a greater _____ of cash if you want to buy that car.

8   The _____ of noise at the concert was very high.

9   I expect there will be a greater _____ of accidents on the roads this year.

10   The _____ of food we will need for the party will increase if you are inviting another six people.

Is it "Less" or "Fewer"?

These two words have similar meanings, but are used differently according to the noun in the sentence.

Less

Less is used with **singular** nouns.

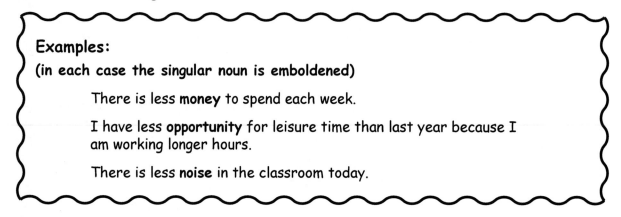

Examples:

(in each case the singular noun is emboldened)

> There is less **money** to spend each week.
>
> I have less **opportunity** for leisure time than last year because I am working longer hours.
>
> There is less **noise** in the classroom today.

Fewer

Fewer is used with **plural** nouns.

Examples:

(in each case the plural noun is emboldened)

> There are fewer **students** taking this examination this term.
>
> Fewer **people** attended the car rally last Sunday.
>
> No fewer than four **countries** may vote.
>
> Fewer **invitations** were sent to invite people to the Proms in the Park this year.

Exercise

Try to put the correct word, "less" or "fewer" in the following sentences.

In the first three sentences the **noun** is emboldened to help you.

TIP: Think what "less" or "fewer" is describing (look for the noun). If it's singular use *less*, if it's plural use *fewer*.

1   I need _____ **help** with my work now I am beginning to understand this subject.

2   There are _____ **jobs** to be done in the office today.

3   The building industry has _____ **employees** than this month last year.

4   It took me _____ time to swim the length of the pool today.

5   I will need _____ than a pint of milk for that recipe.

6   Usually in the post office on Tuesdays there are _____ people in the queue.

7   There are _____ colleges offering language courses this year.

8   I have _____ money than I had last month because I bought a new iPod.

9   Jamil has _____ relatives than Marshall.

10   There are _____ holiday destinations in the brochure and this limits our choice.

Is it "Advise" or "Advice"?

These two words have a very similar meaning as they're both to do with giving and receiving information. Which word has to be used depends upon whether you are receiving information or giving it.

Advise

To advise means to tell or inform someone of something.

Advise is a verb — a "**doing** word" — a word where the word "to" can be put in front of it.

Examples of verbs:

To swim   To hear   To invite   To pounce   To advise

Examples using "advise" and "advised":

I advised him the tyres on his car were flat.

She advised me about how to complete my application form.

I will advise my friend about the best driving school to go to for lessons.

It is easy to advise him; he always listens.

In all these examples someone is **doing** something.

Advice

Advice is some**thing** you give to someone, usually as a result of them asking for your ideas and opinions. (Whether they take your advice is a different matter!!)

Advice is a noun – a word which has in front of it a definite, or indefinite, article.

Examples of definite and indefinite articles:

Definite article	Indefinite article
The computer	An egg
The home	An atmosphere
	A home
	A field

Examples using "advice":

> The **advice** I will give you is not to buy that car.

> Any **advice** I give you I know you will ignore.

> The best **advice** I have to offer is to book your holiday early.

In all these examples some**thing** is being given.

TIP: use "c" for nouns
use "s" for verbs

Exercise

Try to put the correct word, "advise" or "advice", in the following sentences. Think about whether something is being given or received, and if you are using a noun or a verb.

1   I need _____ about buying a new car.

2   It's easy to get _____ but it is not always helpful.

3   Please _____ whether I should accept Bob's invitation.

4   When I have a problem with my computer I always ask for Kevin's _____.

5   When Naomi has a problem with her car she asks Ken to _____ her.

6   Unfortunately I am not able to _____ you.

7   When opening a new bank account, it is important to get the right _____.

8   Think carefully before you _____ anyone to stay at this hotel.

9   It's up to you, but my _____ would be not to stay at that hotel.

10   Diana will be keen to _____ you on the benefits of reflexology.

Is it "Practise" or "Practice"?

These two words look very similar, they sound the same, which is why there is so much confusion in choosing which to use, but there is a definite difference in their meanings.

Practise

To practise means to **carry out** or **do**. It is often something you **do** repeatedly to get better at doing something, for example football skills or dance moves.

Practise is a verb — a "doing word" — a word where the word "to" can be put in front of it.

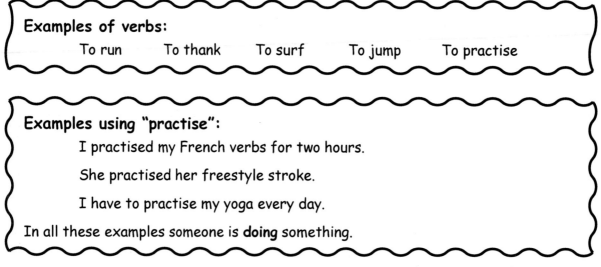

Examples of verbs:

To run   To thank   To surf   To jump   To practise

Examples using "practise":

I practised my French verbs for two hours.

She practised her freestyle stroke.

I have to practise my yoga every day.

In all these examples someone is **doing** something.

Practice

Practice relates to some**thing**.

Practice is a noun — a word which has in front of it a definite, or indefinite, article.

Examples of nouns with definite and indefinite articles:

Definite Article	Indefinite article
The dental practice	A practice manager
The practice building	A practice lap

Examples using "practice":

> The practice of buying fresh vegetables daily is a healthy one.
>
> It is good practice to recycle as much as possible.
>
> In both these examples some**thing** is being described.

TIP: use "c" for nouns
use "s" for verbs

Exercise

Try to put the correct word, "practise" or "practice", in the following sentences. Think if the word is a verb (practise) or a noun (practice).

1 Please _____ your golf swing.

2 You need to _____ your singing if you want to join our choir.

3 The _____ manager is on holiday next week.

4 My dental _____ is closed all day Thursday.

5 Only _____ can help you do something better.

6 It's hard to _____ daily as I am tired after work.

7 I wonder where I can _____ my drumming without disturbing anyone?

8 I always go out when Bob begins his _____.

9 What would you like to _____ today?

10 I don't agree with the _____ of fox hunting.

Is it "Right" or "Write?"

These two words sound the same but they have different meanings.

Right

This word is the opposite of wrong and the opposite of left.

> **Examples using "right":**
>
> It is the right (opposite of wrong) thing to do.
>
> The bank is on the right (opposite of left) hand side of the road.

Write

Write is a verb - a "doing word" - a word where the word "to" can be put in front of it.

> **Examples of verbs:**
>
> To laugh   To study   To think   To write   To invite

> **Examples using "write":**
>
> Ask Sonja to write to the bank.
>
> I have to write my letter of application.
>
> In these examples someone is **doing**, or about to **do**, something.

Exercise

Try to put the correct word, "right" or "write", in the following sentences.

1   I know I am _____ in saying the train is delayed.

2   It's always best to _____ a letter of complaint, rather than to make
       a telephone call.

3   If it's on the _____ then it must be on the same side of the road as
       the post office.

4   Please _____ to your Aunt Phillida. She is waiting to hear from you.

5   Edwin is someone who always wants to be _____.

6   Klaus was unable to _____ as he broke his arm last week.

7   _____ or wrong, it no longer matters.

8   That statement does not sound _____. Please _____ it out
       again.

9   I _____ with my left hand, but it would be _____ to say I
       cannot find any scissors I can use easily.

10   He knew he had to _____ to accept the invitation he had received.

Is It "Took" or "Taken"?

Took

Took is the past tense of the verb "to take".

"Took" is used in the past tense, as in the examples below.

Examples using "took":

I took care of my grandfather when he came out of hospital.

I took some tablets last night to help cure my migraine.

I took the CD back to the shop as it did not play.

Taken

Taken is also the past tense of the verb "to take". But it is used after the words have and had and has.

So you do not say "I have took (or tooken) the train to London", but "I have taken the train to London."

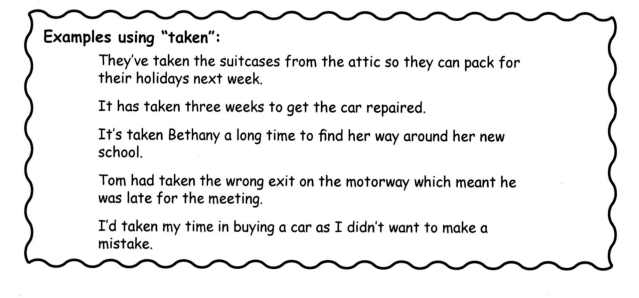

Examples using "taken":

They've taken the suitcases from the attic so they can pack for their holidays next week.

It has taken three weeks to get the car repaired.

It's taken Bethany a long time to find her way around her new school.

Tom had taken the wrong exit on the motorway which meant he was late for the meeting.

I'd taken my time in buying a car as I didn't want to make a mistake.

Exercise

Try to put the correct word, "took" or "taken", in the following sentences.

1   Kai _____ the letter to the post box.

2   It has _____ all day to paint my bedroom.

3   The car _____ more petrol than usual before its service.

4   My sister _____ my brother to the dentist yesterday.

5   We got to the supermarket without a shopping bag as Neill had _____
       it out of the car when he cleaned it.

6   It's _____ me a long time to decide how many people to invite to
       my party.

7   Mark and Jenny have _____ the same holiday dates in June
       because they are getting married.

8   He has _____ Aunt Simmi to Blackpool for the weekend.

9   I'm surprised it's _____ so long to repair her watch.

10   I had _____ care on the stairs, so I don't know how I fell.

Is it "Sat" or "Sitting"?

Sat

Sat is the past tense of the verb "to sit".

"Sat" is used in the past tense, as in the examples below.

> **Examples using "sat":**
>
> I sat on the chair and waited for my car's service to be completed at the garage.
>
> He sat at the front of the class, only occasionally leaving his chair.

Sitting

Sitting is also the past tense of the verb "to sit".

It is used in a number of ways but it is always used after the words was and were.

So you do not say "I was sat on the train", but "I was sitting on the train."

> **Examples using "sitting":**
>
> Troy and Alec were sitting in the car park waiting for their mother to arrive.
>
> George was sitting in the back of the car when the tractor pulled out in front of it.

Exercise

Read the sentences and decide whether each uses "sat" and "sitting" correctly or incorrectly.

		Correct	Incorrect
1	The children were sat quietly during the story.	☐	☐
2	They were sitting on Edinburgh Station when there was an announcement cancelling their train.	☐	☐
3	The journalist was sat at the back of the room during the interview.	☐	☐
4	I was sitting near the front at the concert.	☐	☐
5	He was sat too close to the speakers and found the noise intolerable.	☐	☐
6	The guests were sat in reception for over an hour.	☐	☐
7	"I cannot believe he was sat there for over an hour."	☐	☐
8	Diana and Jillian were sitting in the living room when the lightning struck their television aerial.	☐	☐
9	Susan's dog sat quietly waiting for his supper.	☐	☐
10	I was sat looking at the swans swimming in the lake.	☐	☐

Is it "Lose" or "Loose"?

Lose

Lose is a verb - a "doing word" - a word where the word "to" can be put in front of it.

Examples of verbs:

To dance   To sing   To lose   To invite

Lose means to misplace, to be unable to find.

Examples using "lose":

I was not happy about lending Eleanor my mobile phone as I was sure she would lose it.

Jon always seems to lose any argument he has with his sister Heidi.

Loose

Loose is an adjective - a word which describes another word.

Loose means slack or unfastened.

Examples using "loose":

When we go to the beach we always let Driver, the dog, loose as he likes to run along the shore.

I always tie a loose knot in my shoe laces so I can untie them easily.

Exercise

Try to put the correct word, "lose" or "loose" in the following sentences.

1	The string round the parcel was _____ and it came apart before we got it to the Post Office.

2	Craig went to the dentist because he said his tooth was _____.

3	The dentist was not able to save Craig's tooth. He had to _____ it unfortunately.

4	My grandmother gave me her sapphire ring and told me not to _____ it.

5	I had to take the sapphire ring to the jeweller's because one of the stones was _____.

6	I don't want to _____ your friendship.

7	"If that shoelace comes _____, you will trip and fall", warned Hedley's mother.

8	The airline managed to _____ Lewis' suitcase when he flew back from Paris.

9	I will not lend you the money because I cannot afford to _____ it.

10	The curtain rail was _____ and it fell off the wall.

To "Borrow" or to "Lend"?

These two words are very different, yet there is some confusion as to which should be used. Remember this, you can't borrow something unless it has been lent to you!

Borrow

Borrow = from

Borrow relates to something you have temporarily **from** someone.

Borrowed is the past tense of the verb to "borrow".

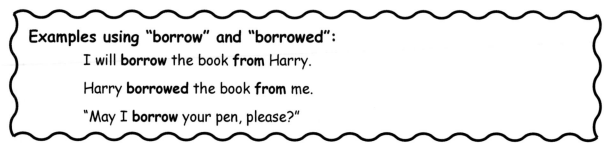

Examples using "borrow" and "borrowed":

> I will **borrow** the book **from** Harry.
>
> Harry **borrowed** the book **from** me.
>
> "May I **borrow** your pen, please?"

Lend

Lend = to

Lend is something you temporarily give **to** someone.

Lent is the past tense of the verb to "lend".

Examples using "lend" and "lent":

> I will **lend** the book **to Benny**.
>
> Benny **lent** the book **to** me.
>
> "Would you **lend** me your pen, please?"

Exercise

Try to put the correct word, "borrow(ed)", "lent" or "lend(s)", in the following sentences:

1   Ask Mr Jones next door if I can _____ his ladder.

2   If Mr Jones _____ me his ladder I can repair my roof.

3   Remember if you _____ something, always give it back.

4   "I am sorry, I cannot _____ you my car."

5   I was asked to _____ him my mobile phone, but I refused.

6   "May I _____ your mobile phone please?"

7   If I was to _____ you money, I know you would ask again and again.

8   I _____ my father's car to meet mother from the station.

9   Geoff could _____ Keith his motorbike, but he is not going to.

10   "Just don't ask to _____ anything else; you never give it back."

NOTE: In some of the previous pages, an example of the verb to "invite" has been included.

We say we "invite" someone to a wedding and use a sentence like this one "I will invite Jonas and Erica to my daughter's wedding."

The word invitation is a noun. A word which is an object like a cheque, a cat, a mobile phone. So we cannot say we will send an invite (a verb) to someone. We must say we send an invitation. It is correct to use invitation in the following ways:

       "I will send Tom and Jack an invitation to Saul's 21st birthday party."

       We have had an invitation to Saul's 21st birthday party.

Be careful how you use these two words.

To "Teach" or to "Learn"?

Teach

To teach is to give knowledge. Someone is the teacher.

Teach is a verb - a "doing word" - a word where the word "to" can be put in front of it.

Examples of verbs:

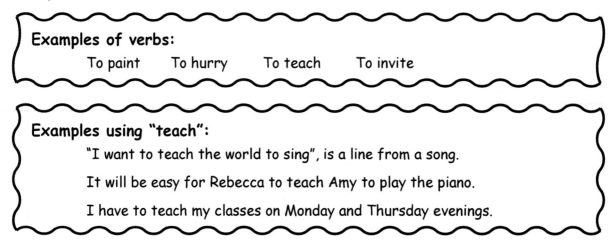

Examples of verbs:

       To paint   To hurry   To teach   To invite

Examples using "teach":

    "I want to teach the world to sing", is a line from a song.

    It will be easy for Rebecca to teach Amy to play the piano.

    I have to teach my classes on Monday and Thursday evenings.

Learn

To learn is to gain knowledge. Someone is the learner.

Learn is a verb - a "doing word" - a word where the word "to" can be put in front of it.

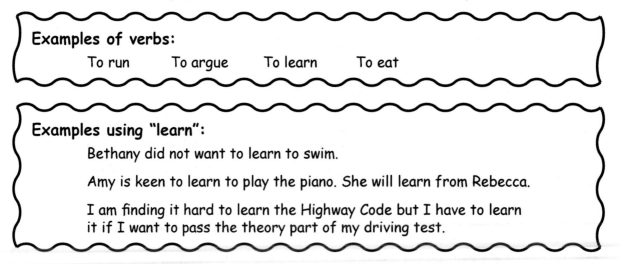

Examples of verbs:

       To run   To argue   To learn   To eat

Examples using "learn":

    Bethany did not want to learn to swim.

    Amy is keen to learn to play the piano. She will learn from Rebecca.

    I am finding it hard to learn the Highway Code but I have to learn
    it if I want to pass the theory part of my driving test.

Exercise

Try to put the correct word, "teach", "taught" (the past tense of the word teach) or "learn", in the following sentences:

1   I will _____ to swim, it's just that I don't like deep water.

2   Please _____ Ruby how to knit.

3   Troy is going to _____ to play the bagpipes.

4   Niall asked his Head of Department to let him _____ his class in

        another room.

5   Who can Troy ask to _____ him to play the bagpipes?

6   Iain is only three years of age but his father is going to _____ him

        to ride a bicycle.

7   Yvonne wants to _____ how to dance properly and needs to find

        some ballroom dancing classes she can attend.

8   I know a school which will _____ Yvonne ballroom dancing.

9   The older you get the less easy it is to _____ a new skill.

10   My mother _____ me to drive. It was not an easy skill for me to

        _____.

Is it "Went" or "Gone"?

Went

Went is the past tense of the verb "to go".

"Went" is used in the past tense, as in the examples below.

> **Examples using "went":**
>
> I went to the auction but did not manage to buy anything.
>
> Tanya went home early because she was unwell.
>
> Sonja went to the dentist for her six-monthly check.

Gone

Gone is also the past tense of the verb "to go", but it is used after the words have and has.

So you do not say "I have went shopping", but "I have gone shopping."

> **Examples using "gone":**
>
> She has gone to see her aunt who has just come out of hospital.
>
> They've gone to the airport to meet Uncle Timmy.
>
> Jasmine's gone to London by train as she got a cheap ticket on the Internet.

Exercise

Try to put the correct word, "went" or "gone", in the following sentences:

1   I _____ to Blackpool for the weekend.

2   He has _____ to his friend's house to use his computer.

3   It's easy to see where the money's _____.

4   It is time he _____ to see his sister.

5   Tony has _____ to take his dog, Jess, for a walk.

6   Tamsin and I _____ to the airport to meet Uncle Jack.

7   She's _____ to Madrid to a wedding.

8   Uncle Jack's flight was late and he thought we'd _____ home and not waited for him.

9   Sanjeep has _____ home early as he is unwell, so I don't know if he _____ to the post office for me.

10   I've _____ there every year for the last three years and this year I want to go somewhere different.

Do I Use "Of" or "Have"?

Of

"Of" is an example of a preposition. A preposition describes the relation between one word in a sentence, and another.

> **Examples of prepositions:**
>
> at   under   with   before   on   after   of
>
> In each of the following sentences think about what is describing the relationship between objects, or people and objects. The first two are described for you with the preposition underlined
>
> We stood <u>at</u> the bus stop. This describes the relationship between **who** was standing **where**.
>
> The man found his briefcase <u>under</u> the car seat. This describes the relationship between the **briefcase** and the **car seat**.
>
> Mark sat at the table.
>
> I will play with baby to keep him quiet.
>
> The London train will arrive before the train from Cheltenham.
>
> The man on the platform is my uncle.

Have

Have is a verb - a "doing word" - a word where the word "to" can be put in front of it.

> **Examples of verbs:**
>
> to stutter   to mutter   to shave   to have

Sometimes, because have and of sound similar, "of" is used wrongly when "have" should be used.

Correct	Incorrect
They should have refused his help. They should've refused his help.	They should of refused his help.
(Remember 've represents the word "have" - Refer to "Apostrophes" on page 4.)	

Correct	Incorrect
I would have thought these sums were easy for you. I would've though these sums were easy for you.	I would of thought these sums were easy for you.

Exercise

Try to put the correct word, "have" or "of", in the following sentences:

1   I would _____ gone to meet her at the station.

2   You should _____ asked me to meet her train.

3   It ought to _____ been an easy task to do.

4   Maybe it will be _____ interest to Reena.

5   Eleanor was suspected _____ lying to her teachers.

6   The post could _____ arrived at any time whilst I was not at home.

7   It really is _____ no importance to me.

8   The dog is vicious and could _____ bitten the boy.

9   Kim clearly shouldn't _____ refused to pay the parking fine.

10   Because she refused to pay the parking fine she ought to _____ been fined.

Is it "Have" or "Get"?

You are in a café, at the counter, and have decided to have a cup of coffee. Which of the following two sentences is correct?

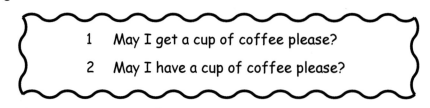

1   May I get a cup of coffee please?

2   May I have a cup of coffee please?

Not sure? Both are correct? Read on . . .

You say, "May I get a cup of coffee?", and the waitress replies, "No, you can't come round here I'm sorry, but I'll get your coffee for you and bring it over if you want to sit at a table."

You are in a shop to buy a birthday present for a friend. You decide on a scarf but would like it in red, not the green one which is on display. You say to the shop assistant, "Can I get this one in red please?" and he replies "No, sorry, we keep them in the stock room and you are not allowed in there. I will go and get it for you."

Have you got the idea now?

Think about whether you are going to do the getting, or someone else is going to get it for you.   If you use "get" it is assumed you will do the getting. If this is not what you mean then use the verb "have".

"May I have a café latté please?"   (Will you get it for me.)

"Do you have this scarf in red?" (Will you look and get it for me.)

"May I get the box from the top shelf?" (You will reach the box and not expect someone to do it for you.)

Exercise

Read the sentences and decide whether each uses "have" and "get" correctly or incorrectly.

		Correct	Incorrect
1	"Would you get breakfast ready for me please, as I am in a hurry this morning and cannot spare the time to do it?"	☐	☐
2	To waitress: "May I get a pizza Italiano and a glass of coke please?"	☐	☐
3	"Can I get the bus into the town from here?"	☐	☐
4	"Whilst I am in town can I get you anything?"	☐	☐
5	"Is there anywhere in town where I can get fresh bread?"	☐	☐
6	To shop assistant: "Can I have a packet of mints please?"	☐	☐
7	To directory enquiries operator: "Would you get me the number for Sunny Destinations Travel in Harwich, please?"	☐	☐
8	To bar staff : "Can I get the same order again please?"	☐	☐

"Able" or "Ible"?

These are suffixes that mean the same thing, i.e. that may be done. For example, visible means may be seen, or laughable which means may be laughed at.

...... able

...... able is a **suffix** (something added to the end of a word).

You would **normally** add **able** if the original (root) word is a word on its own.

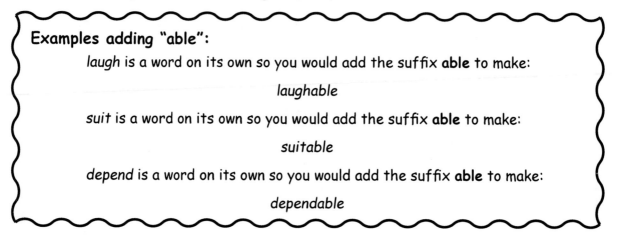

Examples adding "able":

laugh is a word on its own so you would add the suffix **able** to make:

laughable

suit is a word on its own so you would add the suffix **able** to make:

suitable

depend is a word on its own so you would add the suffix **able** to make:

dependable

...... ible

.... ible is a **suffix**.

You would normally add **ible** if the original (root) word is **not** a word on its own.

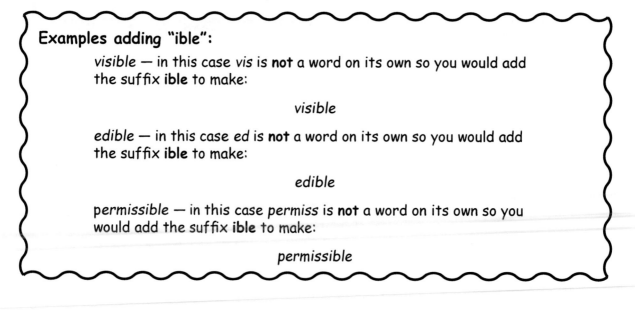

Examples adding "ible":

visible — in this case vis is **not** a word on its own so you would add the suffix **ible** to make:

visible

edible — in this case ed is **not** a word on its own so you would add the suffix **ible** to make:

edible

permissible — in this case permiss is **not** a word on its own so you would add the suffix **ible** to make:

permissible

What do you do when the original word ends in the letter **e**?

It is **usual** when the root words ends in the letter **e**, to drop the **e** and add the suffix.

Examples of words where the letter e has to be dropped:

advise	becomes	advisable
value	becomes	valuable
desire	becomes	desirable
debate	becomes	debatable

Remember, the English language has exceptions to rules (times when the "normal" rules don't apply). If in doubt and when faced with an unfamiliar word —

USE YOUR DICTIONARY.

Exercise: Am I Able............?

Decide which word of the following pairs is spelt correctly. Place a tick ✓ next to the correctly spelt word, **then find that word in the grid below:**

comfortable	☐	comfortible	☐
fashionable	☐	fashionible	☐
incredible	☐	incredable	☐
laughible	☐	laughable	☐
possible	☐	possable	☐
suitable	☐	suitible	☐
terrable	☐	terrible	☐
kissible	☐	kissable	☐
valuable	☐	valueible	☐
visable	☐	visible	☐

```
E L B I S I V W M I E L Q H W
S G V Z D Q Y V H G L A E F B
K U U N F E I K V A B U O R H
F S I F B A V H R H A G K E A
F Q S T H B S M J U U H J L I
X N N D A K Z H Y I L A K B A
N X D U I B I G I F A B R I A
Q V P C Y N L S X O V L H S G
D V J S E T W E S U N E J S F
E L B I R R E T P A O A N O Q
E L B I D E R C N I B V B P J
C O M F O R T A B L E L O L B
E V X A L U A Z X V G T E Q E
V W G J A K Q J W J J Q T U Y
J K Q N R U W Y M K C B U P N
```

Some Words Sound Alike, but...

The Difference Between "Stationary" and "Stationery"

Two words that sound and look very similar, but have very different meanings.

Stationary

This word means "standing still".

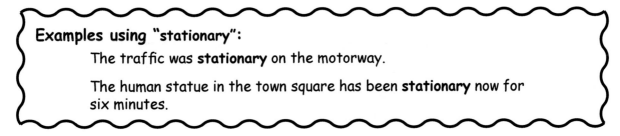

Examples using "stationary":

The traffic was **stationary** on the motorway.

The human statue in the town square has been **stationary** now for six minutes.

Stationery

This word is associated with writing materials, paper and envelopes.

Examples using "stationery":

The **stationery** cupboard contains paper, pens and envelopes.

Ask Trudie to make a list of the office **stationery**.

Tip: remember "e" for "e"nvelopes – **envelopes are** station"e"ry.

Is it "All" or "Al"?

Here are some words which mean different things, and are written in different ways, depending upon whether they have one 'l' or two.

All ready

All ready is used when you want to show you are prepared for something.

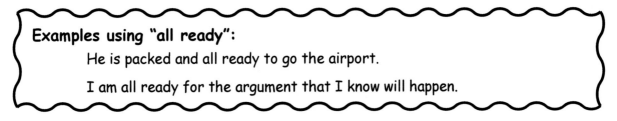

Examples using "all ready":

He is packed and all ready to go the airport.

I am all ready for the argument that I know will happen.

Already

This is used when you want to talk about time that has past.

> **Examples using "already":**
>
> I got to the market but it had already closed.
>
> Monica has already passed her driving test.

All together

These words are used when you want to talk about a summary, or a whole.

> **Examples using "all together":**
>
> All together there were 175 students present.
>
> All together, I have £1,700 worth of savings in two accounts.

Altogether

This is used when you mean completely or entirely.

> **Examples using "altogether":**
>
> It is altogether (*entirely*) a different problem we now face.
>
> I find the whole subject altogether (*completely/entirely*) confusing.

All right

This should be thought of as the opposite of "all wrong" and, as such, is two separate words.

> **Examples using "all right":**
>
> **All right**, I am coming to help you.
>
> It is **all right** to ask Toni if you can share her text book?
>
> It will be **all right** once we settle into the new school.

A lot

"A lot" is the opposite of "a little", and as such, is two separate words.

> **Examples using "a lot":**
>
> Maria has **a lot** of books in her bedroom.
>
> There are **a lot** of people who live in poverty in the United Kingdom.

"Any one" or "Anyone"?

Any one

These words are used when you want to talk about an item in a group of things.

> **Examples using "any one":**
>
> **Any one** of these paint colours would suit your kitchen.
>
> Take **any one** of these pens in order to complete the form.

Anyone

This means "any person at all".

> **Examples using "anyone":**
>
> I do not want **anyone**, other than friends, at my party.
>
> If **anyone** can help me, I will be pleased.

Some Spelling Rules You Just Have to Learn

Sometimes there are spelling rules that you must learn.

Words which end in "e" lose the "e" when "ing" is added.

> **Examples:**
>
> | | | | | | | | |
> |---|---|---|---|---|---|---|---|
> | Complete | Completing | Have | Having | Make | Making | Take | Taking |
> | File | Filing | Love | Loving | Smile | Smiling | Tile | Tiling |

The Plural Rule for Nouns Ending in "y"

See if you can spot the rules about words which end in "y" becoming "ies" when they become plural from the words in the list below. Clue: look at the letter immediately before the "y".

Alley	Alleys	Fly	Flies
Baby	Babies	Galley	Galleys
Boy	Boys	Hobby	Hobbies
Carry	Carries	Jetty	Jetties
Chimney	Chimneys	Monkey	Monkeys
Copy	Copies	Pony	Ponies
Family	Families	Balcony	Balconies

THE RULE

When a word ends in "y" and has a *vowel* before it (a, e, i, o or u), then just add the letter "s".

When the word ends in a "y" and has a *consonant* (any letter other than a vowel) before it, then change the "y" to "ies".

"Full" or "Ful"?

What do you think is the rule relating to the following words?

Beautiful	Beautifully	Careful	Carefully
Faithful	Faithfully	Peaceful	Peacefully
Successful	Successfully	Regretful	Regretfully

THE RULE

When adding "ful" to a word USE ONLY ONE "L" – FUL.

When changing "ful" into "fully" USE TWO "L"s.

The Suffixes "ly" and "ment"

What do you think is the rule relating to the following words?

Accurate	Accurately	Desperate	Desperately
Separate	Separately	Achieve	Achievement
Replace	Replacement	Settle	Settlement
Sincere	Sincerely	Acknowledge	Acknowledgement

THE RULE

When adding "ly" or "ment" to words which end in "e" – keep the "e" in its place.

Exercise: I Can Find the Right Words

Decide which word of the following pairs is spelt correctly. Place a tick ✓ next to the correctly spelt word, **then find that word in the word search below.**

trolleys ☐ trollies ☐ positively ☐ positivly ☐ ☐
advertisment ☐ advertisement ☐ removeing ☐ removing ☐ ☐
loveing ☐ loving ☐ sincerely ☐ sincereley ☐ ☐
bodys ☐ bodies ☐ storys ☐ stories ☐ ☐
cheerfully ☐ cheerfuly ☐ flakeing ☐ flaking ☐ ☐
hopeing ☐ hoping ☐ statement ☐ statement ☐ ☐
hopeful ☐ hopefull ☐

Word Search

```
T E S L O Y I H M Y L S B I Z D
S N W I X M O E L L L G Q W Y N
Y S E F N P S L M S Z F N C K K
E Z V M E C U S T A T E M E N T
L G Z F E F E V R R B L W B E R
L Q U A R S X R P X O R O N E F
O L E E L U I R E V Q D N M G L
R K E A X W D T I L I C O I N A
T H D Z V R N N R E Y V U P I K
C U Z C C L G Y S E I S T D P I
K D G M A U M T M N V P M Q O N
M C V D J K G A G N R D J E H G
S T O R I E S V S V M F A W P T
P O S I T I V E L Y V D Q A A T
Q D Y M A J G V M O X A L K Q L
U V C F F V V E E N A Z W J V M
```

Speaking Skills

Most of the previous hints and tips have been related to, but not exclusively connected with, your writing skills.

When you speak it is equally important to be clear about your meaning so the listeners understand your points.

The following pages contain tips that can help you speak confidently and correctly.

Of course each of these tips should be considered in your writing skills too!

Collective Nouns

It is a trend today for speakers to refer to groups of everything and anything as "bunches". I am sure you have all heard the phrase, possibly even used it, "a bunch of friends", or "a bunch of ideas".

Don't use the word "bunch" to describe a collection of anything except keys, grapes or flowers.

Here is a list of some long-standing and accepted collective nouns:

A pride of lions	A herd of cows	A library of books
A clump of trees	A flight of stairs	A bunch of flowers
A crew of sailors	A company of actors	A string of racehorses

Can you think of a collective noun for a collection of CDs? Possibly a "noise" of CDs!

How about a "ring" of mobiles?

Verb Tense Accuracy

What's wrong with this text?

The open air concert is being held next Friday and Saturday night in the park. The engineers, who are skilled at their job, is installing the loud speakers and public address systems that are being used by the bands and the organisers.

1   **being** is present tense. You say you are being cheeky, or he is being annoying. Yet the concert will take place in the future (next Friday and Saturday).

The correct tense to use is future tense. Hence you should write:

     The open air concert is **to be** held next Friday and Saturday night in the park.

2   **is** installing. Look at the sentence carefully. Who is doing the installing? The engineers.

If this is not easy to see, then read the sentence, missing out the phrase separated by the commas because the fact they are good at their job just gets in the way and is extra information you can do without.

Now it reads   *The engineers is installing* ....

Engineers is plural so the phrase should be:

                     The engineers **are** installing ....

Put back the section separated by commas (that extra information you can do without) and the sentence reads

                     The engineers, who are skilled at their job, are installing ....

3   **are being used** by the bands ....

As we discovered at the beginning of the paragraph, the concert is to be held in the future.

So the bands are **not** using the loudspeakers **now** as now is the present tense.

The sentence needs to reflect the future tense so you should write:

                     public address systems that **will be used** by the bands and organisers.

Exercise

Try to correct the following sentences:

1   Whilst Melanie sits in the garden, the door bell rang.

2   The family hopes the plan to build a new home in the Algarve would work.

3   If the bicycle breaks, he would have to buy a new one.

4   By the time the cricket match started, everyone is thinking England will lose.

5   Hundreds of people will see the exhibition by the time it closed next week.

6   The Members of Parliament, whose average age is 48, is going to Brussels next week by EuroStar.

7   My garden has a number of hedgehogs, mainly in June and July, which is lovely to see.

8   Everyone thinks the plan, thought up by Bill and Trent, are likely to succeed.

9   The students, and their teacher, is trying Functional Skills for the first time this year.

10   Hamill wants to show his friends the photographs he takes on his holiday last year.

Almost the Last Word

Don't be tempted to pepper what you say with words such as "like", "basically", "actual/actually", totally; "amazing", "awesome", etc.

You've all heard expressions such as:

"It was – **like** – raining this morning. I was – **like** – soaked through."

Clearly it was raining and the person was soaked and to suggest that it was like itself is silly. Don't use "like".

"I was – **like** – going up to town."

You are either going to town or not. Don't use "like".

"He was – **basically** – just helping me out."

What you mean is "He was helping me out." Don't use basically, it adds nothing to the sentence and annoys the listener.

"**Basically** – it's my fault."

"It's my fault" is sufficient.

"I was going to the – **actual** – station."

As opposed to the "virtual" station?

"I was actually pleased."

Why use "actually", saying you were pleased is clear enough.

"I'm totally tired." "It's a totally stupid idea."

You are either tired or not tired, totally adds no extra meaning to the sentence.   It is either a good or a stupid idea, "totally" is unnecessary.

What do you mean if you say "I totally care about this topic"?

Amazing means **greatly surprising**. It is used correctly in a sentence such as "After the jumbo jet crashed into the Pacific Ocean the rescuers found it amazing that 150 people were alive in the sea."

So using amazing in a sentence like "Her dress was amazing" or "The concert was amazing" is incorrect.

Awesome means **causing wonder, breathtaking** or **inspiring dread**. It is used correctly in a sentence such as "The volcano erupted with awesome power".

So using awesome in a sentence like "It was an awesome song" is incorrect.

And Finally . . . .

Do think about what you say, the words you use and the message you want to convey.

Do **care** about what you say, the words you use and the message you want to convey.

For this Functional English Level 1 qualification you will need to show you can be clear and accurate in what you say and write, this means expressing your points of view effectively whether written or spoken.

Now is a good time to take a quick look at some of the commonly misspelt words (page 65).

They are included so you can refer to them quickly, but don't forget to also use your very good and indispensable friend **your dictionary**.

Commonly Misspelt Words

This list of commonly misspelt words is included so you can refer to them quickly, but don't forget to also use your very good and indispensable friend **your dictionary**.

Word	word with different ending(s)	Word	word with different ending(s)
A		Attach	Attaching
			Attachment
A lot		Attention	
Absent	Absence	Avenue	
Absolute	Absolutely	Awful	
Accident	Accidental	Axis	Axes
Accommodate	Accommodated		
	Accommodating	**B**	
	Accommodation		
Accompany	Accompanied	Bachelor	
	Accompanies	Balance	Balancing
	Accompanying		Balanced
Account	Accounting	Bargain	Bargaining
	Accounted		Bargained
	Accountable	Beauty	Beautiful
Achieve	Achievement	Before	
	Achieving	Begin	Beginner
Acknowledge	Acknowledging		Beginning
	Acknowledgement	Believe	Believer
Across			Believing
Activity	Activities	Benefit	Benefited
Address	Addresses		Benefiting
	Addressing	Bicycle	
Advertise	Advertising	Borrow	Borrower
	Advertisement		Borrowing
Afraid		Brake	Braking
After	Afterwards	Break	
Again	Against	Brilliant	Brilliantly
Agree	Agreeing	Build	Building
	Agreement		Builder
	Agreeable	Bulletin	
All right		Burglar	Burglary
Already		Business	
Altogether		Buy	Buying
Amend	Amending		Buyer
	Amendment		
Amount	Amounting		
	Amounted		
Appear	Appearing		
	Appearance		
Article			

Word	word with different ending(s)	Word	word with different ending(s)
C		Desperate	Desperately
			Desperation
Calendar		Detached	
Calm	Calming	Develop	Developing
Careful	Carefully		Development
Carriage		Dial	Dialled
Catch	Catching		Dialing or Dialling
Category	Categories	Diary	
Central		Different	Differently
Centre	Centred		Difference
Charge	Charging	Disappear	Disappearance
Chief	Chiefly		Disappearing
Choose	Choosing	Double	Doubled
Chose	Chosen		Doubling
Close	Closing	Draw	Drawing
	Closure	Drawer	
		Duly	
Colleague			
College		**E**	
Compare	Comparison		
	Comparatively	Edge	Edging
Competent	Competently	Eight	Eighth
Complete	Completely		Eighteen
Compliment	Complimentary	Eighty	
Correspond	Corresponding	Electric	Electricity
	Correspondence		Electrical
Create	Creating	Elegant	Elegantly
	Creation		Elegance
Crescent		Embarrass	Embarrassing
			Embarrassingly
D			Embarrassment
		Enter	Entering
Data			Entrance
Decent	Decently	Environment	Environmental
Decide	Deciding		Environmentally
	Decision		Environmentalist
Defend	Defence	Example	
Definite	Definition	Except	Exception
Delete	Deleted		Exceptionally
	Deleting	Excite	Excitement
Deliberate	Deliberately		Exciting
Depend	Depending	Exercise	
	Dependable	Exhibition	
Descend	Descending	Expect	Expecting
	Descendant		Expectation
Deserve	Deserved	Expense	Expensive
	Deserving	Experience	
		Extreme	Extremely

Word	word with different ending(s)
F	
Facility	
Fail	Failing
	Failure
Familiar	Familiarly
Favourite	Favourable
February	
Figure	Figuring
Final	Finally
Foreign	Foreigner
Fortune	Fortunate
	Fortunately
Forty	
Fourteen	
Friend	Friendly
	Friendliness
Fulfil	Fulfilment
	Fulfilling
Furniture	
G	
Garage	
General	Generally
Gold	Golden
Govern	Governing
	Government
	Governor
Grammar	Grammatical
	Grammatically
Graph	
Guarantee	Guaranteeing
	Guarantor
Guard	Guarding
H	
Half	Halve
Height	
Heir	Heirloom
Hero	Heroes
Humour	Humouring
	Humorous
	Humorously
Hungry	Hungrily

Word	word with different ending(s)
Hygiene	Hygienic
	Hygienically
I	
Idea	
Identical	Identically
Immediate	Immediately
In between	
In fact	
In front	
Income	
Indeed	
Independent	Independently
	Independence
Innocent	Innocently
	Innocence
Insert	Inserting
	Insertion
Install	Installing
	Instalment
	Installation
Intelligent	Intelligence
	Intelligently
Intention	Intentional
Interest	Interesting
	Interested
Involve	Involving
	Involvement
J	
Jealous	Jealously
Jewel	Jewels
	Jeweller
	Jewellery
Join	Joining
Journey	Journeying
Judge	Judging
K	
Keen	Keenness
Keep	Keeper
	Keeping

Word	word with different ending(s)	Word	word with different ending(s)
Key	Keying	Mirror	Mirroring
	Keyboard	Miscellaneous	
Kind	Kindness	Month	Monthly
Kiosk		Most	Mostly
Knife	Knives	Move	Moving
Know	Knowing		Movable
	Knowledge		Movement
	Knowledgeable	Multiple	Multiply
		My	Myself

L

Labour	Labouring
Laid	
Language	
Leave	Leaving
Legal	
Leisure	Leisurely
Library	Librarian
Lighten	Lightening
Like	Likely
	Liking
	Likelihood
	Likewise
Lonely	Loneliness
Loose	Loosely
	Loosen
Lose	Losing
Lovely	
Luxury	Luxurious

M

Magazine	
Main	Mainly
Maintain	Maintaining
	Maintenance
Manage	Managing
	Management
	Manageable
Marvel	Marvellous
Mathematics	Mathematician
Meant	
Menu	
Message	Messaging
	Messenger
Minute	

N

Nature	Natural
Near	Nearly
	Nearby
Necessary	Necessarily
	Necessitate
	Necessity
Negative	Negatively
Negotiate	Negotiating
	Negotiation
Neighbour	Neighbourly
	Neighbourhood
Nerve	Nervous
	Nervously
New	Newly
	Newness
Ninth	
No one	
Noise	Noisily
Notice	Noticing
	Noticeable
Nowhere	

O

Object	Objecting
	Objection
Occasion	Occasional
	Occasionally
	Occasioned
Occupy	Occupying
	Occupier

Word	word with different ending(s)	Word	word with different ending(s)
Occur	Occurred Occurring Occurrence	Quarter	Quarterly Quartering Quartered
Odour	Odourless	Question	Questioned Questioning Questionable
Offer	Offered Offering		
Often		Questionnaire	
Omit	Omitting Omission	Queue	Queuing
		Quick	Quickly
Opinion		Quiet	Quietly
Opportunity	Opportunities	Quite	
Ordinary	Ordinarily	Quiz	
Original	Originally Originate	Quotation	
Owe	Owing		

R

		Word	word with different ending(s)
		Rare	Rarely
		Reach	Reaching
		Ready	Readily
		Real	Really Reality

P

Word	word with different ending(s)
Particular	Particularly
Pay	Paying Payment
Perhaps	
Permanent	Permanently
Permit	Permitting Permissible
Persuade	Persuading
Phase	Phasing
Prejudice	Prejudicial
Prepare	Preparing Preparation
Present	Presence
Probable	Probably Probability
Procedure	
Profession	Professional
Prompt	Prompting Promptly
Proof	Prove
Public	Publicly
Punctuate	Punctuation
Pursue	Pursuing

Reason	Reasoning Reasonable
Receive	Receiving
Reception	
Recognise	Recognising
Recommend	Recommending Recommendation
Refer	Referred Referring Referral
Referee	Reference
Register	Registration
Repeat	Repeating Repetition
Reply	Replying
Responsible	Responsibility Responsibly
Restaurant	
Reverse	Reversing Reversible
Rough	Roughly
Route	Routing

Q

Word	word with different ending(s)
Qualify	Qualifying
Quality	
Quantity	

Word	word with different ending(s)	Word	word with different ending(s)
S		**U**	
Salary		Umbrella	
Salutation		Union	
Scene	Scenery	Unnecessary	Unnecessarily
	Scenic	Until	
Secret	Secretly	Unusual	Unusually
Secure	Securely	Use	Useful
	Security		
Sentence		**V**	
Separate	Separately		
Sign	Signing	Value	Valuable
	Signature	Vary	Various
Similar	Similarly		Varying
	Similarity		Variable
Sincere	Sincerely	Vegetable	
	Sincerity	Villain	Villainous
Six	Sixth	Virtual	Virtually
Speak	Speaking	Visible	Visibly
	Speech		Visibility
Special	Speciality	Visible	Visibility
Success	Successful	Volunteer	Volunteered
	Successfully		
Surprise	Surprising	**W**	
System	Systematic		
	Systematically	Waste	Wasteful
			Wastage
T		Wednesday	
		Weird	
Tariff		Whole	Wholly
Teach	Teacher		Wholesome
	Teaching	Wield	Wielding
Temperature		Wilful	Wilfully
Temporary	Temporarily		Wilfulness
Tempt	Tempting	Withhold	
Tend	Tendency	Without	
Ticket		Wool	Woollen
Tomorrow			
Tongue		**Y**	
True	Truly		
Truth	Truthful	Yacht	Yachting
	Truthfully	Yesterday	
Try	Tries	Yield	Yielding
	Trying	Your	Yourself
Twelfth			Yourselves
Type	Typical		

SECTION 2

HOW DO I ....?

The skills you will need to learn and in which you will have to become competent in order to gain this Functional Skill qualification are described on page 1.

The skills are covered in the practice tasks in Section 3.

The Reference Sheets in this section provide opportunities for you to review and practise the skills for Functional English Level 1.

Arranging Text in Alphabetical Order

> **In this section you will learn how to:**
>
> 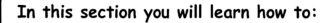 present information in a logical sequence (W1.2)

You will be required from time to time, at work, in your studies and for your personal use, to arrange information in **ascending** or **descending** alphabetical order.

The Alphabet

A B C D E F G H I J K L M N O P Q R S T U V W X Y Z

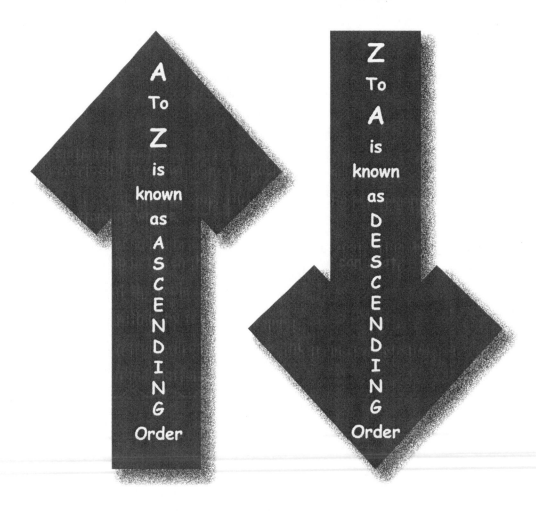

How Do You Arrange a Simple List?

Look at the following first names that are to be written in alphabetical order.

Neil, Albert, Christopher, Mark, Sebastian, Phillip, Jack, Oswald, Liam

Here's How

Look at the **first letter** of each word then arrange the words to they follow the order of the letters of the alphabet.

Neil, Albert, Christopher, Mark, Sebastian, Phillip, Jack, Oswald, Liam

Following the alphabet the names are arranged thus:

Albert, Christopher, Jack, Liam, Mark, Neil, Oswald, Phillip, Sebastian

How do you arrange names which start with the same letter?

Look at the names in the list. Some of them begin with the **same** letter.

Neil, Norman, Arthur, Albert, Clark, Christopher, Declan, Daniel, Oswald, Oliver, Peter, Phillip, Liam, Leonard, Steven, Saul, Evan, Eric.

Here's How

Look at the **first letter** and then look at the **second** letter of the word and follow the order of the alphabet.

Neil, Norman, Arthur, Albert, Clark, Christopher, Declan, Daniel, Oswald, Oliver, Peter, Phillip, Liam, Leonard, Steven, Saul, Evan, Eric.

Albert and Arthur will be the first two name in the list and Albert will be placed first because the second letter "l", in Albert, comes before the second letter, "r" in Arthur.

Do this with the rest of the list and you should end up with the list looking like this:

Albert, Arthur, Christopher, Clark, Daniel, Declan, Eric, Evan, Leonard, Liam, Neil, Norman, Oliver, Oswald, Peter, Phillip, Saul, Steven.

Arranging first names and surnames into alphabetical order

Look at this table of names.

First Name	Surname
Lucy	Holcroft
Aimee	Plant
Bradley	Ladderman
Tina	Sutton
Rebecca	Masters
Ruby	Manners
Troy	Ingles

How would you arrange these into alphabetical order?

When dealing with lists of names where you have first and surnames, it is usual to arrange the **surnames** in alphabetical order and write the **surnames** first.

For example:

        Barnes   Amy

        Burton   Jon

        Cavendish   Mark

Did you notice that Barnes came before Burton. Both names begin with the letter B so are arranged according to the **next letter**. In this case Ba comes before Bu.

Now you have a go at arranging the list in the table above. Put the surname first and arrange the surnames into ascending (A to Z) order.

In this example, in some of the words the first two letters are the same. In these cases simply look at the third letter of the word and follow the order of the alphabet.

Answer

Holcroft	Lucy
Ingles	Troy
Ladderman	Bradley
Manners	Ruby
Masters	Rebecca
Plant	Aimee
Sutton	Tina

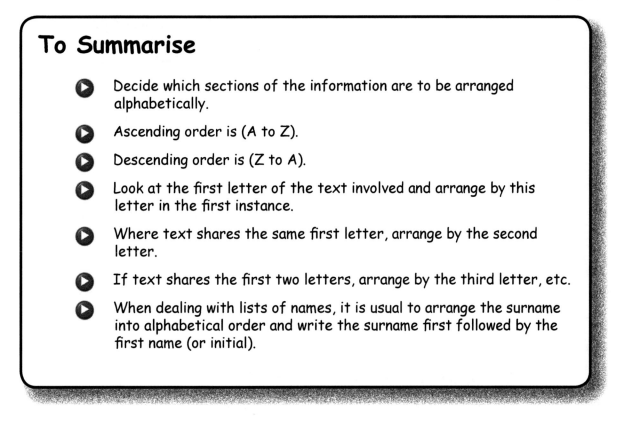

To Summarise

- ▶ Decide which sections of the information are to be arranged alphabetically.

- ▶ Ascending order is (A to Z).

- ▶ Descending order is (Z to A).

- ▶ Look at the first letter of the text involved and arrange by this letter in the first instance.

- ▶ Where text shares the same first letter, arrange by the second letter.

- ▶ If text shares the first two letters, arrange by the third letter, etc.

- ▶ When dealing with lists of names, it is usual to arrange the surname into alphabetical order and write the surname first followed by the first name (or initial).

Completing Forms and Job Application Forms

In this section you will learn how to:

- ▶ identify the main points and ideas (R1.1)

- ▶ understand texts in detail (R1.2)

When completing a form of any type, whether it is a form to open a bank account, a mobile phone account, a student rail card, a passport, a holiday or a job application form, **accuracy** and **neatness** are vitally important.

Before you put pen to paper do the following:

 Study the form, all its questions and sections, so you know what information you will be expected to provide.

 If possible, photocopy the form, and practise filling it in. This will help you judge how large or small your writing should be in order to add the information required. It also shows you what your completed form will look like and help you decide if you can improve how you express your information and present your form.

75

✓ Carry out any research you need for the questions asked. For instance, you may have to provide information that you have stored somewhere; studying the form's questions alerts you to the fact that you need to **find that information**.

When completing the form do the following:

✓ Use **BLACK INK** and **BLOCK CAPITALS** — these guidelines are usually stated on the form and you will be aware of them, having read it carefully and thoroughly before completing it.

✓ Use neat handwriting that is easy to read.

✓ Fill in every section — even if it means putting **Not Applicable** in some sections.

✓ Make sure you answer each question fully.

✓ Make sure you have deleted inapplicable information (usually indicated by an asterisk *) on the form, for instance *delete whichever is not applicable.

✓ Check your spelling is correct.

✓ Be honest.

✓ Keep a copy of the form before you send it off.

You will have to complete a variety of forms throughout your life. These simple guidelines will make that process easier and you will be confident of getting it right and portraying the right image.

Job Application Forms

The tips above apply equally to **job application forms**, but there are some extra points to consider.

Namely:

✓ Research the company carefully. You will probably be asked a question at interview that will check how much you know about the company, its product(s), partners, etc., and your research is vital.

✓ Read the job description carefully so you can be clear about what skills and qualities the employer sees as important. You can then make sure you include information on your application form to support the fact that you have some of these qualities and skills.

✓ Include details of qualifications you have achieved (don't include failures, your application form must concentrate on **positive** aspects).

✓ Confirm, before naming them, who your referees are to be. It is bad manners to quote someone's name as willing to give you a reference if you have not received their permission in the first place. They may refuse to act as referee if you do not clear it with them first.

- Be sure to include a **job reference number** if one was quoted in the advertisement.

- Use sentences rather than just bullet points throughout the form.

- Check, and double-check, spelling, grammar and punctuation.

- Sound positive and enthusiastic.

- Do not lie.

- Take a copy of the form to refer to **before** the interview. You will probably apply for several jobs at the same time and you will need to remember what you said to each prospective employer.

- Return the form **well before the closing date**, and make sure you keep the form **clean, tidy and as uncrumpled** as possible.

The Purpose of Your Neatly, Accurately Completed Job Application Form

A prospective employer, on reading your form, should have a positive idea of the following:

- How your personality and qualities are suited to the job and the company.

- How your qualifications and skills are suited to the job and the company.

- How you have given your application careful consideration.

Completing an Application Form

Have a look at the completed application form to join a health club on *page 79*.

The intention of the form is to gather information such as contact details and additional information that the organisation will find useful, perhaps for marketing.

The reader is asked to complete the form in **CAPITALS**. This is to make the handwriting clearer and easier to read.

How do you set about completing the form?

1   Read the form's headings carefully so you know what information you are asked to include.

2   Gather all your information **before** you begin to complete the form. If you do this you will have everything to hand (bank account details, etc.).

Sometimes, if you don't have all the details to hand when you begin to complete the form you might think to yourself "I'll complete and post it later, when I have the information needed". In many cases (and we have all done this) you will put the form down, find it a day later, forget there is information missing, and post it! Not a good impression to give (particularly if you are applying for a job and have left out details of your qualifications!). **So, gather all your information before you begin to complete the form**.

3   It is sensible to take a copy of the form, if possible, so you can practise filling it in on the photocopy. This will show you if you can get all the information into the spaces provided. If not, you know to make your handwriting smaller.

If you can't take a copy of the form, or get a second copy from the person who issued it in the first place, draft it on a separate sheet. This serves the same purpose and it **will** help when you come to complete the form.

Why is this an important step? Because any form you complete should be done neatly and be free from errors and crossings out. This makes a good impression.

Look at the completed form

Is every section completed?

Is the information included appropriate?

Is it signed?

The Health Club has asked you to select the facilities you are most interested in. Why do you think they have done this?

Well, it could be that they will use this information to advertise these facilities in the future. If they know certain things are popular, this might be one of the things which attracts people to the health club. When they know what is not so popular, they can review these areas in the club and try to make them more popular.

Each piece of information requested on a form is there for a reason.

FIRST STEPS TO FITNESS HEALTH CLUB

Alderley Road   Pevensey Green   Sussex   SX4 9JZ
☎ **01533   670082   www.fstf.health.com**

APPLICATION FOR MEMBERSHIP

Please complete the form in CAPITALS

Name	MIA FLETCHER
Address	16 GATENBY ROAD, BEXHILL ON SEA, SUSSEX SX17 5BE
Telephone Number (Landline):	01535 677882
Mobile:	77645635522
Email address:	miafletcher@bexhill.co.uk
Date Membership to begin:	1ST FEBRUARY 2010

MEMBERSHIP PLAN

Select choice of Membership from the options below

Annual	£250	☐	Half-year	£150	☑	Monthly £40	☐
Family Membership	£200	☐	Quarterly	(3 months)	☐		

AREA(S) MOST LIKELY TO BE USED

Gym	☑	Dance Studio	☐	Swimming Pool	☑
Racquet Halls	☐	Steam Room	☐	Sauna	☐
Health and Beauty Area	☐	Weight Training	☐	Hydro Pool	☐
Exercise Machines	☐	Yoga Classes	☑	Race Track	☑

METHOD OF PAYMENT

I wish to pay for the *HALF YEARLY* Membership at a cost of *£150.00*
by (tick appropriate box below)

Cheque	☐	Credit Card	☐	Visa/Mastercard	☐
Debit Card	☐	Standing Order	☐	Direct Debit*	☑

* Bank Account Details for Direct Debit authorisation

Bank SOUTH EASTERN BANK PLC   Bank Sort Code 38-92-66

Account Name MIA FLETCHER   Account Number 27653489

Writing and Setting Out Memos

A memorandum (abbreviated to memo) - plural memoranda

> ## In this section you will learn how to:
>
>  identify the main points and ideas and how they are presented in different texts (R1.1)
>
>  understand texts in details (R1.2)

A memo is an **internal** method of communication within an organisation.

Memos must be short documents, and usually deal with one subject. A long document within an organisation is usually sent in the form of a report.

The memo should be signed by the sender.

Memo 1

Although organisations have their own style of layout for memos, all memos contain these essential headings:

To

From

Date

Subject

Copies to

MEMORANDUM

Mrs A Winston, Personnel Manager

T Gilbert, Central Records Manager

11 October 2009

Lost file

Mr J Brown, Personnel Director
Miss P Patty, Central Records Clerk

Last week I informed you that Mrs Jane McTavish's file had been lost or mislaid.

I am pleased to report that this has now been found and I have written to Mrs McTavish apologising for the delay in confirming the details she requested.

I am sorry for the inconvenience that this has caused all parties.

Trevor Gilbert

Trevor Gilbert

The subject of the memo has been identified.

This section indicates who else, other than the named recipient, has received a copy.

Typical layout of a memorandum (memo). This is formal as it includes their titles (Mr, Mrs, Personnel Manager, etc.).

The **purpose** of this document is to **give information**. What are the clues?

1   The **first paragraph** has the words "I informed you that......" these are key words that indicate some further information is about to be given.

2   The **second paragraph** gives updated information and the key words to notice are "I am pleased to report ...." at the beginning of the sentence. This indicates to the reader a successful outcome and that some information is about to be given.

3   Another phrase in the **second paragraph** indicating details of action taken is "I have written ......".

All these phrases indicate a document that gives information to the reader.

In this example you can see the message is short and simple and deals with only one point.

Who the memo is from, and to whom it is being sent, are identified and the document is dated and signed.

Memo 2 – another formal memo

MEMORANDUM

To   Jamil Sunni, Car Park Manager

From   Catherine Woodleigh, Personnel Assistant

Date   28 September 2009

Re   Car Parking Arrangements

The new car parking arrangements came into operation on 20 September and I outlined the new procedures in my memo dated 15 August. This memo clearly described the system and the duties you would be required to undertake.

Unfortunately, it has come to my attention that despite my requests, you have not been following my instructions. I have had a number of complaints from staff who have been unable to park in their allotted space because they have found it already occupied. Additionally, some staff have been unable to use the car park as the barrier does not operate with their key card.

This state of affairs is unacceptable and I wish you to attend a meeting with me on Wednesday 30 September at 9.15am with a view to discussing these, and other, problems that have occurred since the introduction of the new system.

Catherine Woodleigh

Catherine Woodleigh

The **purpose** of this document is to **make a complaint**. What are the clues?

1. The **first paragraph** describes the background/topic of the memo.

2. The **second paragraph** uses three key words "**unfortunately**, it has come to my **attention** that **despite**". All these words are rarely used in a document that aims to convey that everything is all right.

3. The **third paragraph** uses the key words "state of affairs is unacceptable" and goes on to give an instruction to attend a meeting at a set day and time, without offering the opportunity of checking this is convenient or rearranging. All these are clues that something is definitely not right.

Clearly, the writer of this document is dissatisfied.

Informal Memo

This is an example of an **informal** memo:

MEMORANDUM

To   Janet Markham, Advertising Department

From   Catherine Woodleigh, Purchasing Department

Date   15 June 2009

Re   Company's Sales Brochure

The 2,000 copies of the company's Christmas brochure have been received from the printer today.

These are available for you to collect at your earliest convenience.

Catherine

In this example, the names have no title and there are no job titles included — although people's departments are shown. This is important because an organisation could employ people with the same name but who work in different departments.

The memo is dated. There is a subject — this time expressed as 're' (short for 'reference').

The memo is signed with the sender's first name only health club the surname could be included.

Taking Messages

In this section you will learn how to:

 identify the main points and ideas and how they are presented in different tests (R1.1)

identify texts in detail (R1.2)

It is always helpful to use a standard message form to record a message, whether it is a telephone message or a message of another kind. The headings on a standard form will help you include the information needed.

There is a message form on the following page, but this is not the only layout that companies use.

Remember you should always:

✓ Use simple, straightforward words.

✓ Keep your sentences short but vary the length a little so that the message reads well.

✓ Include all, **and only, the key facts and information.**

✓ Leave out irrelevant information.

✓ If you are repeating a request for the reader of the message to **do something,** make it a request, **not an order.**

✓ Be very specific and clear about days, dates and times. If you have to give a non-specific time, e.g. "tomorrow", add the day and date in case your message is not read immediately. It is advisable to always be specific about days and dates in order to avoid confusion.

 Mark urgent messages clearly.

Your responsibility does not end when you place the message on the right desk – it only ends when the person has read it and understood it.

Identifying the Key Facts

Every message contains key facts. If you miss them out of the message it will not make sense – or not make **complete sense**.

Business callers are normally quite good at giving the key facts in an ordered way and checking them through afterwards. Private callers may be less helpful and some may like to chat, so that it becomes difficult to sort out what is important from what is not.

A good way to check you have the message clear in your mind is to read back your summary to the caller. This both checks that you have the message correctly with all the important facts, and gives the caller the opportunity to alter or add anything.

TELEPHONE MESSAGE FORM

TO...DEPARTMENT ....

DATE ....TIME..

CALLER'S NAME ....

ORGANISATION ....

TELEPHONE NUMBER ....FAX NUMBER ....

EMAIL ADDRESS..

✓ Appropriate action box(es)

Telephoned	☐
Telephoned	☐
Returned your call	☐
Called to see you	☐
Left a message	☐
Requests you call back	☐
Please arrange an appointment	☐

Message ....

....

....

....

....

....

....

Taken by... Department.................................... Time..................

This is a telephone message that was left late last night on the company's answering machine and that the person listening to the messages will have to pass on to the intended recipient.

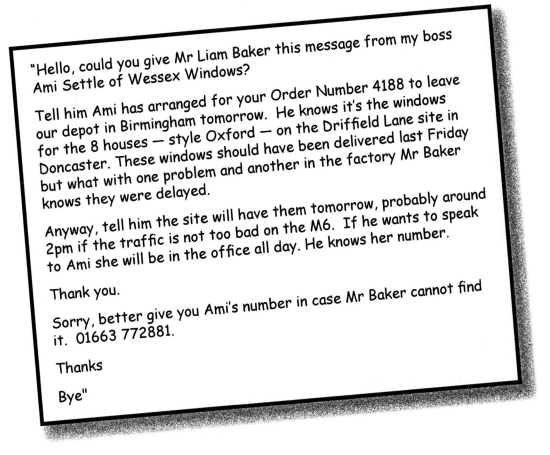

"Hello, could you give Mr Liam Baker this message from my boss Ami Settle of Wessex Windows?

Tell him Ami has arranged for your Order Number 4188 to leave our depot in Birmingham tomorrow. He knows it's the windows for the 8 houses — style Oxford — on the Driffield Lane site in Doncaster. These windows should have been delivered last Friday but what with one problem and another in the factory Mr Baker knows they were delayed.

Anyway, tell him the site will have them tomorrow, probably around 2pm if the traffic is not too bad on the M6. If he wants to speak to Ami she will be in the office all day. He knows her number.

Thank you.

Sorry, better give you Ami's number in case Mr Baker cannot find it. 01663 772881.

Thanks

Bye"

The **important** parts of the message have to go onto the Telephone Message Form.

How will you decide what are the important parts?

1   Study the telephone message form so you know what information **could** be included. Remember that **not every** section of the telephone message form will be appropriate in **every message**.

   In the example there is space for a fax number and an email address. You don't have this information so leave those spaces blank.

2   Study the message and **highlight** or **underline** the important parts. Don't bother with the "interesting" but not important facts. In our message interesting facts are the problems in the factory **and** the fact the windows should have been delivered earlier. The person for whom the message is intended will know this already. You can probably also assume that the person receiving the message knows what the order is for.

3   Not everyone leaves a message that is in a **logical** order. When you have highlighted the important and relevant information:

— think about the information you have that can be placed on the form, and

— think about the order in which you will write the information.

4   Look at how the Telephone Message Sheet has been completed. Would you have added anything else? Do you think all the important facts have been included?

TELEPHONE MESSAGE FORM

TO......*MR LIAM BAKER*..............................DEPARTMENT....*(You don't have this so cannot include anything here)*

DATE *PUT IN LAST NIGHT'S DATE*....TIME *(You don't have this so leave it blank)*

CALLER'S NAME *AMI SETTLE* *(Although Ami did not make the call, you don't know the caller's name and in any case the call was made on behalf of Ami).*

ORGANISATION *WESSEX WINDOWS*

TELEPHONE NUMBER *01663 772881*...FAX NUMBER

EMAIL ADDRESS

✓ Appropriate Action box(es)

Telephoned	☐
Telephoned overnight	☑
Returned your call	☐
Called to see you	☐
Left a message	☑
Requests you call back	☑ *URGENTLY*
Please arrange an appointment	☐

Message

The windows relating to Order Number 4188 will be delivered today

(add the day and date to avoid confusion - DID YOU NOTICE THE MESSAGE WAS LEFT LAST NIGHT AND THE "TOMORROW" MENTIONED IS "TODAY"!!).

The order will leave the Birmingham Depot today and arrive at the

Driffield Lane site in Doncaster, hopefully by 2pm.

If you want to speak to Ami ring her on the above telephone number.

Taken by............................. Department .... Time.............................

Reading and Understanding Information Displayed in Tables

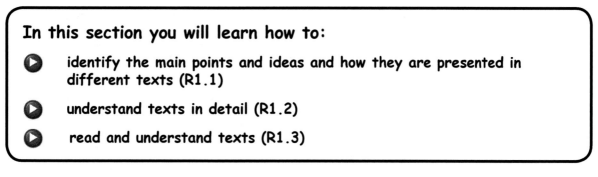

In this section you will learn how to:

▶ identify the main points and ideas and how they are presented in different texts (R1.1)

▶ understand texts in detail (R1.2)

▶ read and understand texts (R1.3)

Information is very often displayed in tables. Think about the holiday brochures you look at when deciding to book a holiday. The tables show information about the hotels and the costs, and you have to be able to understand the information in order to decide if you want to book that longed-for holiday.

In order to make sense of the information presented, there are a number of steps you need to take.

1 Read the **table title** *This tells you what the table is about and appears, usually, at the top of the table.*

2 Read the **column headings** (columns go vertically) *These explain the type of information included in each column.*

Look at the example below:

MP3 PLAYER STATISTICS AND PRICES

Model	Battery Life (hours)	No. of songs	Rechargeable Battery	Built-in USB Plug	Colour(s)	Price
MP3/AA	8	320	No	Yes	Silver	£14.99
MP3/BB	32	320	Yes	No	Black, Silver	£15.99
MP3/BC	21	600	Yes	Yes	Pink, Blue	£25.99
MP3/DD	10	320	Yes	No	Grey	£29.99
MP3/EF	5	20	Yes	Yes	Blue, Red	£29.99
MP3/GG	15	1000	Yes	Yes	Silver, Red	£49.99

The **table title** clearly tells you that the table is about the features of MP3 players and their prices.

The **column headings** indicate you will find information on such things as the Model of MP3 player; the battery life of the MP3 player; the number of songs the MP3 player will hold, etc.

Now look at the table below and answer the questions that follow.

Sam's weekly income and spending

Income	Week No	Spending				Spending Total
		Clothes	Socialising	Toiletries	Sport and Fitness	
£67.10	20	£11.99	£20.00	£10.00	£14.00	£55.99
£73.45	21	£22.50	£15.00	£9.99	£14.00	£61.49
£57.93	22	£9.00	£25.00	£4.99	£14.00	£52.99
£76.00	23	£39.99	£5.00	£5.99	£14.00	£64.98

1   How many types of spending are recorded in the table?

2   In which week did Sam spend the most on clothes?

3   In which week was Sam's income the lowest?

4   What does Sam spend the same amount of money on each week?

5   In which week, and on what item, did Sam spend the least?

ANSWERS

1   In order to answer Question 1 you will have noticed the heading **Spending** then looked beneath it to discover there are **4** types of spending being recorded.

2   The answer to Question 2 is **Week 23**. If you got this right you will have looked at the entries in the "Clothes" column and found that the most Sam spent was £39.99. But in which week did Sam do this? You will have looked at the column headed "Week No" and found that the £39.99 was spent in Week 23.

3   There is a column heading "Income". Reading down this column you will have discovered that the lowest sum of money Sam earned was £57.93 and this was in **Week 22**.

4   To answer this question you will have had to study the entries in all the 4 "Spending" columns. You will have seen Sam spends £14.00 every week and the column heading indicates it is spent on **Sport and Fitness.**

5   To answer this you will need to look at all the money Sam spent on every item. You will have discovered Sam's lowest spend was £4.99. Reading the column heading you will see this was on **Toiletries**. You are also asked to state the **week** when the least money was spent, so you will have looked along the line to the week column to discover this was in **Week 22.**

If you got these questions right it will mean you have begun to learn how to correctly interpret information set out in tables. Well done.

When You Have to Display Information in Tables

Remember the things that helped you understand the information - the table heading and the column headings. Any table you create will have these things so that the person reading your table can understand it.

Reading and Understanding Information Displayed in Charts

In this section you will learn how to:

▶ identify the main points and ideas and how they are presented in different texts (R1.1)

▶ understand texts in detail (R1.2)

▶ read and understand texts and take appropriate action (R1.3)

Information is often displayed in charts. Some people find charts easier to read and interpret than tables, or other methods of displaying information (data).

Look at the example below:

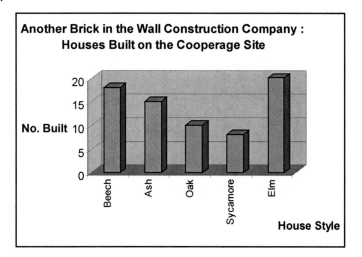

In order to make sense of the information presented, there are a number of steps you need to take.

1 Read the **chart title**. *This tells you what the chart is about and appears, usually, as a heading.*

2 Read **axes** details. *These tell you the names of the House Style (the horizontal axis) and the number of each style of house that has been built (the vertical axis).*

Look at the following chart and try to decide what it is about?

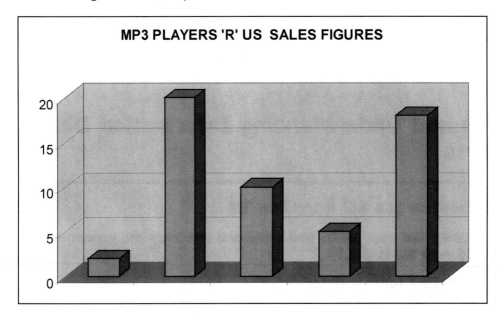

The **title** tells you the chart is about sales figures but the sales of what? Presumably MP3 players as that is in the chart's title. However, this may **not** be the case.

You have no idea what this chart is about because there are no explanations.

Try to answer these questions:

- What period does the "Sales Figures" cover?

- The sales of what items are shown?

- What do the figures represent?

- Is the final column really 17 or is it 17 million?

Now go back to the chart on *page 89* and answer these questions.

1 What type of building is being represented on the chart?

2 How many styles of building are shown on the chart?

3 What is the name of the building company?

4 The company has built the most of which style of building?

ANSWERS

1   In order to answer Question 1 you will have noticed the heading of the chart which includes the company's name and the words **"Houses built ......"**. You are able to detect that the type of building represented is **Houses**.

2   Because the horizontal axis says **House Styles** you know this refers to **Beech, Ash, Oak, Sycamore** and **Elm**, so there are **five** House Styles represented on the chart.

3   In order to answer Question 3 you will have noticed the heading of the chart which includes the company's name **Another Brick in the Wall Construction Company**.

4   The vertical axis is labelled "No. Built". You can see the numbers go from 0 to 20. To answer this question you will have looked to see which of the five "bars" is the tallest. This is the one on the right. Looking on the horizontal axis which names the "house style" you will see this bar relates to the sales of House Style **Elm**.

If you got these questions right it will mean you have begun to learn how to correctly interpret data displayed in charts.

Well done.

Using Images in Communication

In this section you will learn how to:

▶   present information in a logical sequence (W1.2)

▶   Use language, format and structure suitable for purpose and audience (W1.3)

Images can be used to enhance and explain written communications.

Remember, use images **to enhance the text** and to help the reader's understanding of the text. An image may also provide information in addition to text. **An image should not be included if it has no relevance**.

Think carefully about why you are using images and only use appropriate images in appropriate places.

Presenting Numerical Data in Visual Form

It is important to recognise that presenting information in just one way might not suit every reader.

In the first two examples, which present information on temperatures in Europe, some people will find it easier to understand the information in the table, whilst others prefer to see a graph or a chart.

Therefore, the **purpose** of including the chart **and** the table in the document is to allow the reader to interpret the information in the way they can best understand.

Example 1

Data in tabular (table) form

EUROPEAN TEMPERATURES 14 FEBRUARY	
Prague	13
Helsinki	8
Oslo	6
Stockholm	10
Madrid	16
Lisbon	14
Warsaw	7

Example 2

Data in graphical form (a bar chart)

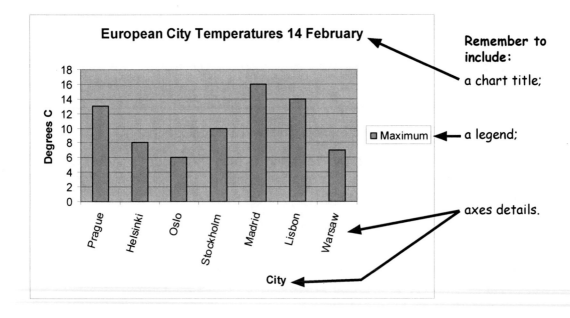

Remember to include:

a chart title;

a legend;

axes details.

Using Images in Text

Advertisement 1

Including an image to attract readers and encourage bookings:

CRUISING ON THE AIDAdiva

Imagine ...... it's 9.30 in the morning and your luxury cruise liner has just docked in yet another picturesque Mediterranean harbour. You have just finished breakfast in one of the three restaurants on the top deck of the vessel and looking out of your cabin window you can see yet another picturesque island waiting to be explored.

The forecast for the day ahead is 27° and you have until your cruise liner leaves port at 9pm to explore today's destination.

Don't leave it to your imagination:

Come and experience the relaxing life on board this newest addition to the AIDA* fleet

Telephone: Sailaway Cruises on 01855 6775520
for full cruising information

* AIDAdiva's sisters include:
AIDAbella. AIDAaura, AIDAcara, AIDAvita, AIDAluna

Advertisement 2

In this instance, the *text* is being used to give additional information about four areas of the country:

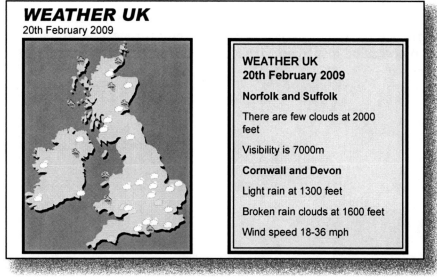

WEATHER UK
20th February 2009

WEATHER UK
20th February 2009

Norfolk and Suffolk

There are few clouds at 2000 feet

Visibility is 7000m

Cornwall and Devon

Light rain at 1300 feet

Broken rain clouds at 1600 feet

Wind speed 18-36 mph

Writing Advertisements

Advertisements may be placed in newspapers or magazines for a number of reasons, including:

- to advertise jobs;
- to promote products or services;
- to announce special events or functions;
- to publicise changes in an organisation;
- to recall faulty goods.

The **classified advertisements** section of a newspaper allows quick reference to a wide range of advertisements, which are usually inserted according to subject.

Line Advertisements

GOOD BUY, BRAND new telephone/fax/
copier/scanner for sale.   Owner is relocating
abroad. Tel: 0184 576399

This information runs from line-to-line, often using the same typeface throughout, with no special layout. Charges are made by the line, normally with a minimum charge for three or four lines.

In such advertisements (also know as lineage ads), an opening should be made that catches the readers' attention, and then as much abbreviated information as possible should be contained in as few lines as possible.

Display Advertisements

These may use a variety of fonts and sizes, and may be illustrated with artwork and colour. Charges are based on the number of column centimetres, often with a minimum size. Information can be displayed within the advertisement to attract attention to special features.

Porto Santo Lines

£35

ONE DAY CRUISE

Discover a new island. Porto Santo Line offers you an unforgettable one-day package, aboard the ship "Lobo Marinho".

Travel with us and find out why Porto Santo is called the "Golden Island". Contact us today to make your reservation.

**Porto Santo Lines, Rua da Praia 6, Funchal, Madeira
Tel/Fax 291 228 662**

Column Advertisements (in newspapers and magazines)

The pages of newspapers and magazines are divided into **columns** and advertisers purchase so many column widths. The publisher charges so much per column and depth of advertisement.

In the following example the page has been divided into four columns. Hop, Skip and Jump has taken an advertisement over two columns.

HOP, SKIP AND JUMP

Shoe manufacturers of quality

END OF SEASON SALE

Leather Uppers • Leather Soles
• Luxury Comfort Linings

Sizes 5, 6, 7, 8, 9, 10 and 11.

Brogue Black	Brogue Brown
Oxford Black	Oxford Brown
Casual Black	Casual Brown
Lace Black	Lace Brown

Telephone to place an order TODAY
Whilst stocks last

0165 7873 9882

Designing Advertisements

Designing an advertisement is an exercise in **summarising**. It is important to pick out the main points, features, advantages, or whatever is relevant to the theme of the advertisement.

It is essential to ensure the advertisement will be **seen** on the page of the newspaper or magazine. If it is displayed unattractively, it will not achieve this objective. Here are some guidelines:

 Use a company logo, prominently displayed. People can identify with a well-known logo.

 Whatever is being advertised, display the headline **PROMINENTLY** using bold text, underlining, or **ALL CAPITALS**, for instance.

 Break up the information sensibly and logically; perhaps various points could be listed using an asterisk or a bullet point.

 Use spacing and balance sensibly — remember the more space you use the more you will pay!

 Try to achieve a progressive display that categorises information logically, leading finally to action required by the reader — "visit us on ???" "contact us", etc.

Writing and Setting Out Business Letters

In this section you will learn how to:

- ▶ identify the main points and ideas (R1.1)

- ▶ write clearly and coherently including an appropriate level of detail (W1.1)

- ▶ present information in a logical sequence (W1.2)

- ▶ use language, format and structure suitable for purpose and audience (W1.3)

- ▶ use correct grammar including subject/verb agreement and correct and consistent use of tense (W1.4)

- ▶ ensure written work includes accurate grammar, punctuation and spelling and that the meaning is clear (W1.5)

A business letter is an **external** method of communication and reflects how an organisation communicates with, and is viewed by, people and organisations outside the business.

There are a number of purposes for business letters:

- ✓ providing information;

- ✓ giving instructions;

- ✓ confirming arrangements;

- ✓ improving customer services;

- ✓ public relations.

A business letter has three parts:

1   introductory paragraph;

2   middle paragraph(s);

3   closing paragraph.

Introductory Paragraph

The introduction/opening paragraph introduces the theme/purpose of the letter and puts it into a context or provides a background.

Introductory paragraphs are also used to mention essential people, events or things to which the letter will refer.

Middle Paragraph(s)

These provide detailed information.

The middle paragraphs of a letter **develop a theme** and **provide all relevant details** and particulars. The number of paragraphs used will depend upon the complexity of the letter's subject. However, paragraphs should be kept fairly short and deal with only one topic at a time. **New topic = new paragraph** is something you must keep in mind.

Closing Paragraph

This provides an action statement and a courteous close.

In this paragraph you will attempt to summarise your comments and state what action you will take, or wish to be taken.

Some letters are concluded with a courteous sentence to act as a means of signalling the end of the document.

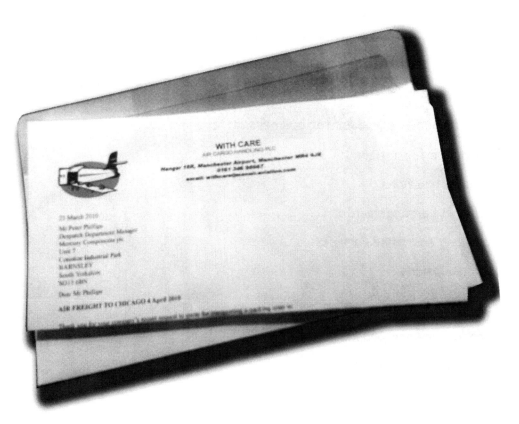

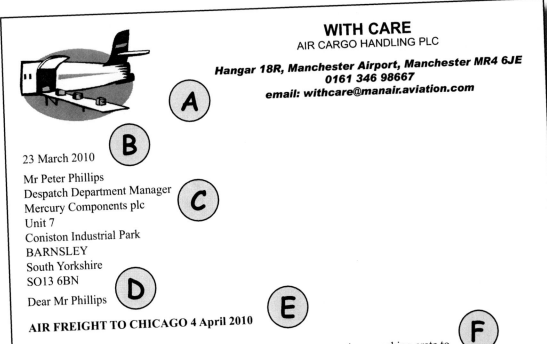

WITH CARE
AIR CARGO HANDLING PLC

Hangar 18R, Manchester Airport, Manchester MR4 6JE
0161 346 98667
email: withcare@manair.aviation.com

Ⓐ

Ⓑ

23 March 2010

Mr Peter Phillips
Despatch Department Manager
Mercury Components plc
Unit 7
Coniston Industrial Park
BARNSLEY
South Yorkshire
SO13 6BN

Ⓒ

Dear Mr Phillips Ⓓ

Ⓔ

Ⓕ

AIR FREIGHT TO CHICAGO 4 April 2010

Thank you for your company's recent request to quote for transporting a packing crate to Chicago.

As you know, our Mike Richards came to your organisation yesterday to examine the crate, take its measurements and establish its weight. As a result of his visit we are pleased to be able to quote the sum of £568.90 + VAT. Our formal quotation is enclosed with this letter.

For this sum we will: Ⓖ

- collect the crate on 2 April before 12 noon
- transport it to our depot at Manchester Airport
- ensure the paperwork for its journey is in order
- obtain UK Customs clearance for the crate
- put it on flight WC457 departing at 15:20 hours on 4 April, for Chicago O'Hare Airport
- upon arrival, arrange for our American handlers to unload the crate and obtain US Customs clearance
- store safely in the depot until your US client collects the crate.

We trust this quotation is acceptable and look forward to assisting you on this occasion. We would need confirmation of your wish to employ our services no later than 28 March. Ⓗ

If you wish to discuss this matter further, please do not hesitate to contact me.

My direct line number is 0161 346 2323.

Yours sincerely Ⓘ

Paul Falcon
Procurement Manager
Enc

Ⓙ

Key to Parts of a Business Letter

(A)   The **letter heading** of the company including a company logo.

(B)   **Date** expressed as dd/mm/yyyy.

(C)   **Name**, **title** and **company name** and **address** of the person and company receiving the letter.

(D)   **Salutation** – Dear Mr Phillips because the letter is addressed to him in the name and address line.

(E)   **Heading**: indicating what the letter is about.

(F)   **Introductory paragraph**.

(G)   **Middle paragraphs** providing details.

(H)   **Closing paragraphs** providing an action statement and a courteous close.

(I)   **Complimentary close**: Yours sincerely because the recipient's name is used in the salutation. The writer's name and title, leaving space for his signature!

(J)   **Enc** indicating there is an enclosure.

Useful Phrases for Business Letters

Thank you for your letter dated ....

As you may know, ...

I wish to inform you that ....

I was pleased to hear that ....

I wish to enquire about ....

I should like to place an order for ....

I look forward to hearing from you in the near future.

I should be grateful if you would kindly send me ....

Following our recent telephone conversation, I wish to ....

Please do not hesitate to let me know if I can do anything further to help ....

Business Letter 1

SETHCOTE STATIONERY AND COMPUTING SUPPLIES

Sethcote House: Bamfield Way: YOUR TOWN YW3 5BK

01662 4522128   www.sethcote.stationery.co.uk

17 March 2010

Mr I Curlish
7 Pine Ridge Road
YOUR TOWN
YW14 5BP

Dear Mr Curlish

Thank you for your recent enquiry concerning the photo quality paper we stock at Sethcote Stationery and Computing Supplies.

We are pleased to give you the details you have requested.

We have the following products available:

Gloss A4 size	packet of 20 sheets	£6.49
Matt A4 size	packet of 100 sheets	£7.99
Satin A4 size	packet of 20 sheets	£6.50
Gloss 6 x 4 size	packet of 20 sheets	£1.99
Matt 6 x 4 size	packet of 50 sheets	£2.50

For those customers who find it inconvenient to come into the store, we offer a next-day postal delivery service for all our paper products at the quoted cost, **plus** £2.50 postage and packing.

If we can be of any further assistance please do not hesitate to let us know. We look forward to being of service to you.

Yours sincerely

Seth Cotefield

Seth Cotefield

The **purpose** of this document is to **give information**. It also states facts. What are the clues?

1   The **first paragraph** has the words "Thank you for your recent enquiry". This gives a clue that the person receiving this letter has been asked for information and that **this** document being written will contain information.

2   The **second paragraph** uses the key words "We are pleased to give you details". Once again, this indicates the letter will give information.

3   The purpose of the document is to give information to someone who understands the subject – in this case paper quality and sizes. The writer has presented the information on the paper prices in a style that is easy to follow and that stands out from the other text of the letter. The recipient is able to see, at a glance, the main information that was requested. The information is sufficiently detailed to give the customer information on various products from which he can make a choice.

In this way the document meets the **purpose** and the **audience**.

4   **Paragraph four** gives additional information that the customer may not have known and may find useful. This information is used to **persuade** the customer to buy.

5   **Paragraph five** is a polite way of ending a letter that gives information and is also a way of creating an impression of being helpful, together with encouraging custom. The key words are "If we can be of any further assistance", "please do not hesitate to let us know", and "we look forward to being of service to you".

The information the letter contains has been arranged in a logical sequence. It begins by stating the purpose of the letter, it then gives details which were requested. It goes on to give further information which might be of interest to the reader, and then it closes with the offer of further help.

> NOTE: The letter uses "we" throughout. It is important not to begin with "we" (the company or organisation) then change to "I" (the writer) half way through. You must *be consistent*.

Business Letter 2

BROOKFIELD BOROUGH COUNCIL

15 April 2009

The Proprietor
Painted Ladies Hair Stylist
66 High Road
YOUR TOWN
YV5 4GG

Dear Madam

It has come to the attention of this Council that you have placed a notice in the first floor windows of the property you occupy at 66 High Road, Your Town. This notice covers all three windows facing the High Road and acts as an advertisement for your business.

Unfortunately this notice contravenes the local by-law 55c (sub-sections 9 – 12), which clearly states that business names and details must only be displayed on the **ground floor** and above the shop doorway(s). Accordingly this letter gives you notice to remove the offending addition to your property **no later than 10am on 25 April**. Failure to comply with this request will result in your business being fined the sum of £2,200 per day for each day the notice remains after 25 April.

A copy of the relevant by-law is enclosed for your information.

Yours faithfully

J Allan

J Allan
Assistant Solicitor

Enc

The **purpose** of this document is to **give information and request a necessary course of action.** It also states facts. What are the clues?

1 **Paragraph 1** begins with the phrase "It has come to the attention ....". This phrase rarely means the reader will hear anything good. In this case the reader is about to receive a warning. The phrasing of the letter is very formal – which means polite but to the point and allowing no room for negotiation.

2 **Paragraph 2** contains a further clue with the word "unfortunately", which rarely means good news.

3 The information is presented clearly and logically because the first paragraph states the nature of the problem and the second paragraph details why it is a problem, giving information about what must be done, by when and what will occur if this action is not taken.

NOTE: It is important in your writing that the subject and the verb agree.

An example of this is the wording in Paragraph 2 — "Unfortunately this notice contravenes the local bylaw 55c (sub-sections 9 — 12), which clearly **states** that ...." You might think "states" should be "state" because "state" agrees with "sub-sections". However, this would be incorrect.

Here is it important to look at what the word "states" relates to. The sentence could be written as "Unfortunately this notice contravenes the local by-law 55c, which states that ....". It is the by-law 55c that states something.

Using the Telephone and Making Telephone Calls

Before You Place a Call

✓ Think about what you wish to say and how you will say it. Courtesy is expected when using the telephone just as if you are talking in person.

✓ Make a list of what you need to say and the information you need to give and/or receive **before placing the call. BE PREPARED.**

✓ Dialling too quickly may be the cause of dialling a wrong number. Never just hang up. Apologise and let the person who answered the telephone know you have dialled the incorrect number.

How to Speak on the Telephone

✓ When speaking, think of the way you sound. On the telephone sounds and moods are magnified. **Talk with a smile in your voice.** The person on the other end of the telephone cannot see your facial expressions and your tone of voice will need to express politeness, enthusiasm and efficiency.

✓ Make sure you say your words clearly and precisely. It is embarrassing, and time-wasting, to be asked to repeat what you are saying. Names and addresses are particularly difficult, so say yours slowly, spelling any unusual words.

Making Telephone Calls

It is polite, and necessary, to identify yourself. If you are calling from a company, then you would need to identify your company, your name, and perhaps your department, before going on to say why you are calling. For instance:

Good morning, this is Blackwood and Company of York. Janet speaking from the Purchasing Department. I am ringing to place an order...... I wish to speak to ....

How to Answer a Ringing Telephone

The proper way to answer the telephone is give a greeting – **hello; good afternoon** - followed by identifying your telephone number if it is your home, or your name and your company. **Never** answer with just "hello" or "yes". Hello is useless because it does not tell the caller anything, and "yes" is curt and impolite, and again it does not tell the caller anything - except perhaps that you are in a bad mood and cannot be bothered.

Good Manners on the Telephone

Answer a ringing telephone promptly.

If you dial a number that is wrong, apologise promptly and hang up.

Calling a business at or very near closing time is thoughtless and not likely to result in a successful call.

Introduce yourself when placing a call.

Answer a phone by identifying yourself, your company and/or your department.

When speaking to anyone who is working and for whom time is important, make your call informative and short – plan ahead.

It is polite to let the person who **made** the call **end** the call.

Sending Faxes

Facsimile Transmission

A fax is an efficient and speedy method of communication and can be used to send text and images. However, there are some important points to consider when sending a fax.

When and What to Fax

Always make sure the message is clear and take into account the following:

 Only send faxes when communication is **URGENT**. Email would be another suitable method of urgently communicating something, but a fax can be used when someone does not have email.

 Don't count on privacy – remember that it is not always the case that the person to whom the fax is being sent has their own fax machine. Most companies have centrally placed fax machines. For this reason be aware that the message can be seen and read by anyone. Do not send sensitive or confidential information in this way.

Always use a **Fax Cover Sheet**. It should contain the following information:

 The receiver's name and fax number.

✓ Your name, your business name, address, telephone number and fax number.

✓ The date (and possibly time).

✓ The total number of pages being transmitted, including the cover sheet. When you list the number of pages, it means the recipient can check that all pages have been received.

✓ A list of what you are faxing to ensure that the other party receives everything you've faxed.

✓ Cover sheets may also include special notations, such as "Urgent" and "For Immediate Delivery".

Some things do not fax well:

✓ Limit the use of dark colours as they increase transmission time and use the recipient's ink!

✓ Do not use light colours for text as they may not be seen by the fax machine as dark enough to register.

✓ Try to avoid colour images and photographs in faxes.

Fax Cover Sheet

Clearly mark who the fax is **to**. (If the company to which you are sending the fax has a centrally placed fax machine, make sure the fax gets to the right person by clearly identifying the recipient's name and job title.)

Include the **fax number**. (If your company has a central fax machine, it may not be you who sends the fax, but a telephonist. Make sure she/he can see the fax number clearly.)

FAX COVER SHEET

To:	Henry Henderson, Manager	**Fax No:**	01904 768257
From	Pamela White, Sales Manager	**Fax No:**	01904 768299
	White and Green Brothers	**Time:**	Time sent
Date:	Date sent	**No. of Pages**	
Re:	Subject of the fax		

FAX INCLUDES: Fax cover sheet and 2 pages. The second page includes a bar chart.

☐ **Urgent**   ☐ **Please comment**   ☐ **Please reply**   ☐ **Please acknowledge receipt**

White and Green Brothers 18 Park Gate Mews Salford Quays
Manchester MA13 5GY
0161 372 2236

Give your name.

Include your fax number.

Remember to count the front cover as page 1.

Writing and Setting Out Personal Letters

In this section you will learn how to:

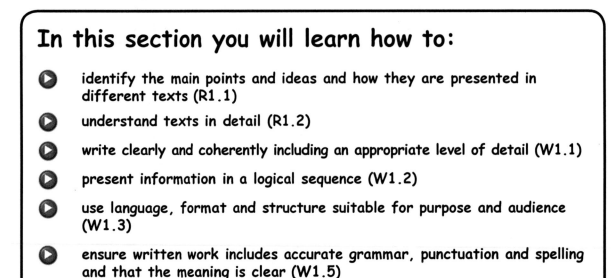

- identify the main points and ideas and how they are presented in different texts (R1.1)

- understand texts in detail (R1.2)

- write clearly and coherently including an appropriate level of detail (W1.1)

- present information in a logical sequence (W1.2)

- use language, format and structure suitable for purpose and audience (W1.3)

- ensure written work includes accurate grammar, punctuation and spelling and that the meaning is clear (W1.5)

A personal letter is a letter written from someone's home address to either:

- a company – for instance to accompany a job application, or to complain about something; or

- a friend – for instance to invite a friend to stay with you.

Some Points to Remember About Letter Writing

- **Firstly: the date.**

  Put the date the letter is written. This date should be shown as: dd/mm/yyyy

that is: 14th June 2009. Do not mix this order.

- **Secondly: the name and address to where the letter is being sent.**

  Remember to write to a person if you can;

that is: Mr Jaz Allahan.

> If it is an informal letter to a friend, it is acceptable to omit the name and address.

If you don't know the name of the person, address the letter to a job title;

that is: The Marketing Manager.

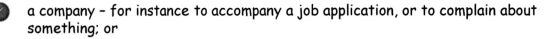

REMEMBER: Don't just write Allahan and Corby Ltd. A COMPANY cannot open a letter, but a PERSON can!

Thirdly: who are you writing to?

When you write "Dear ...." it is called the salutation.

When you write "Yours ...." it is called the complimentary close.

The salutation and complimentary close must match;

that is:
Dear Mr Jones = Yours sincerely

Dear Sirs = Yours faithfully

When you use a person's name, be sincere!

Note: Only the word *Yours* has a capital letter at the beginning.

 Fourthly: sign the letter.

A letter from you needs to be signed. After the complimentary close, leave yourself space for a signature, then print your name. This is important because your signature may not be readable and the person who receives the letter will not know your name.

In an informal letter to a friend you can write "Dear Patrick".

If it is an informal letter to a friend you just need to write "Best wishes" or "Kind regards" and sign your first name.

Examples of Address, Salutation and Complimentary Close

Name and address:	Mr P Marks Sunningbrow Golf Course Sunningbrow Hill Aberdeen AB7 3NH
Salutation:	Dear Mr Marks
	Never write Dear Mr P Marks – just Dear Mr Marks. Think of how you would address him if meeting him. You would say "Mr Marks", so write it as you would say it.
Complimentary close:	Yours sincerely
	You have used his name, so be SINCERE!

Name and address:	The Sales Manager McKie and Aston plc 8 School Fields York YO14 5ND
Salutation:	Dear Sir or Madam
	because you have not used a name
Complimentary close:	Yours faithfully
	You have not used a name, so how can you be SINCERE!

Name and address:	Mrs K Trent Office Manager T&N Agency Villamoura Road Bexhill on Sea Sussex SX5 7BQ	**This time you have used a name and a job title.**
Salutation:	Dear Mrs Trent	
	because you have addressed the letter to her	
Complimentary close:	Yours sincerely	
	You have used her name, so be SINCERE!	

110

A Personal Letter Written to a Company

> ## In this section you will learn how to:
>
> ▶ identify the main points and ideas and how they are presented in different texts (R1.1)
>
> ▶ understand texts in details (R1.2)
>
> ▶ present information in a logical sequence (W1.2)
>
> ▶ use language, format and structure suitable for purpose and audience (W1.3)

Letter 1

The following is an example of a personal letter written to a company:

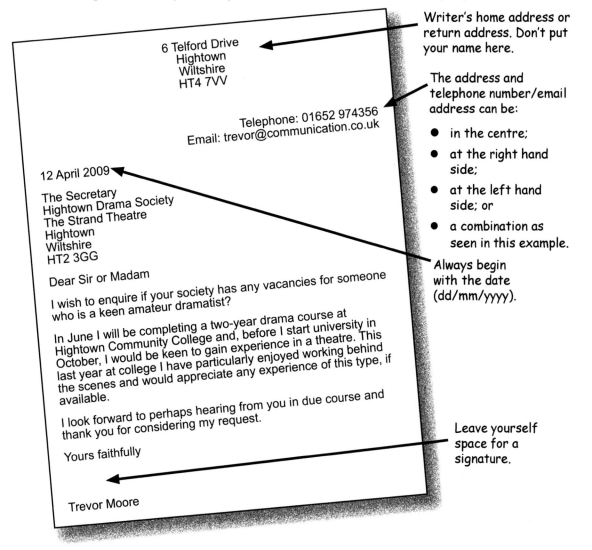

6 Telford Drive
Hightown
Wiltshire
HT4 7VV

Telephone: 01652 974356
Email: trevor@communication.co.uk

12 April 2009

The Secretary
Hightown Drama Society
The Strand Theatre
Hightown
Wiltshire
HT2 3GG

Dear Sir or Madam

I wish to enquire if your society has any vacancies for someone who is a keen amateur dramatist?

In June I will be completing a two-year drama course at Hightown Community College and, before I start university in October, I would be keen to gain experience in a theatre. This last year at college I have particularly enjoyed working behind the scenes and would appreciate any experience of this type, if available.

I look forward to perhaps hearing from you in due course and thank you for considering my request.

Yours faithfully

Trevor Moore

Writer's home address or return address. Don't put your name here.

The address and telephone number/email address can be:

● in the centre;
● at the right hand side;
● at the left hand side; or
● a combination as seen in this example.

Always begin with the date (dd/mm/yyyy).

Leave yourself space for a signature.

What do you think was the main purpose of Letter 1?

Was it to give information? Was it to ask for information? Was it to apply for a job?

It was mainly to make an enquiry about vacancies which might be suitable for Trevor Moore. The clue for the reader is in the **first paragraph** with the phrase used at the very beginning, "I write to enquire". Immediately the recipient (the reader) knows they will have to respond to the letter because it asks a question.

The writer has stated **in the first paragraph** the purpose of the letter and the nature of the enquiry. This presents the information **clearly and logically**.

In the second paragraph the writer goes on to **persuade** the reader why this enquiry should be looked upon favourably because he gives information about his experience and interests that are relevant to his enquiry. This aims to persuade the reader he is suitable and that Hightown Drama Society cannot do without Mr Trevor Moore!

The words in the **final paragraph** that indicate a response is expected are "I look forward to perhaps hearing from you ....". It would be impolite for the drama society not to acknowledge the letter.

So, if you want a reply to a letter you write, consider using the same words as Trevor.

An Informal Personal Letter to a Friend

In this section you will learn how to:

▶ write clearly and coherently, including an appropriate level of detail (W1.1)

▶ present information in a logical sequence (W1.2)

▶ use language, format and structure suitable for purpose and audience (W1.3)

Letter 2

The following is an example of an informal personal letter written to a friend:

Writer's home address, or return address. Don't put your name here. →

Middlebank Farm
Trum Gelli
Gynedd
GY11 15MK
Wales

07751345 678
pigriffiths22@farmstead.co.uk

The address and telephone number/email address can be:

● in the centre;

● at the right hand side;

● at the left hand side.

9 June 2009

Dear Molly

I received your letter just today, even though you posted it first class on 2nd June!

It was great to hear all your news. I imagine you are quite excited about being chief bridesmaid for Julia. Fortunately your sister has consulted you about the colour and style of dress and, I must say from your description, it sounds lovely – not too embarrassingly fussy!

Mother and father say to send their best wishes to Julia for 2nd July, and of course they wish her and Graeme a happy married life.

Once the wedding is over you must come and stay for a few days before we fly to Mauritius in August. Just let me know and we'll arrange to meet you at the station.

I've lots to tell you but it can wait until I see you in August. I don't suppose you have thought of what you are going to take to Mauritius, whereas I have metaphorically packed and unpacked my case dozens of times!

See you soon.

Best wishes

Pam

Leave yourself space for a signature.

This letter is a personal letter to a friend. It is 'chatty' but still uses good grammar, spelling and punctuation. **Do not be tempted to use abbreviations like you use in text messaging.**

The language is less formal than the other letters you have so far read in this book, but what Pam wishes to convey to Molly is structured logically.

The **first paragraph** takes the form of a general, informal greeting between friends.

The **second paragraph** talks about a forthcoming wedding that Molly is attending as bridesmaid.

The **third paragraph** sends good wishes to Molly's sister from Pam's parents.

The **fourth and fifth paragraphs** move logically to plans for after the wedding.

The **final paragraph** is a brief, friendly "See you soon" greeting.

It's acceptable to be informal between friends but you would not phrase a formal letter in this way.

Writing Reports

In common with any other business document, a report needs to be planned and, before beginning, you must consider the following:

 A report will usually be requested by people who need the information for a specific purpose.

 A report differs from an essay in that it is designed to provide information that will be acted on, rather than to be read by people interested in the ideas for their own sake. Because of this, it has a different structure and layout.

 Do not write in the first person.

 Use the past tense to describe your findings.

"It was found that.......... etc., etc.". **It** rather than **I** and the past tense of the verb to find, i.e. **found.**

Points to Consider Before Beginning your Report

For whom am I writing the report?

 A named individual, or a group of people?

 Person(s) who have no knowledge of the subject matter?

 What do the readers need to know?

 What do the readers already know?

What is my objective?

- To inform the readers?
- To explain ideas?
- To persuade?
- To consult?
- To transmit ideas or information, facts or findings?
- To make recommendations about ways of doing things, making improvements or changes?

What is the context?

- Urgent/important?
- Routine or "one-off"?
- Stand alone, or linked with a presentation?
- Sensitive?

What source material?

- Is it readily available?
- Do I need to do any research?

If you skip the planning stage, poor preparation invariably causes time-consuming problems at a later stage.

Structuring a Report

A report is used for reference and is often quite a lengthy document. It has to be clearly structured for you and your readers to quickly find the information it contains.

Parts of a Report

The nature of the report will vary from routine reports to complex, non-routine reports. The layout will vary too, yet all reports should have the following common features:

Cover Sheet

This should contain the following:

- full title of the report;
- your name;

the name of the person(s) for whom the report is intended;

  the date.

Terms of Reference

This refers to:

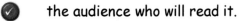 the main subject of the report;

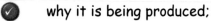 the scope and purpose of the report;

 the audience who will read it.

The terms of reference should tell you:

  what the report is going to discuss;

  why it is being produced;

  who will read it.

You need to know this information before you begin the process of producing the report:

what? + why? + who? = terms of reference

Title

When you have established the **terms of reference** you can consider the **title**.

For any title to be of value it must:

  reflect the terms of reference;

  be precise and refer directly to the subject of the report.

Main sections/findings

The report will need to be divided into various logical sections and sub-sections. Make full use of **paragraph headings** and **paragraph numbering** including **bullet points**.

This is the section in which you:

  state what you found out;

  clearly present your results, making use of paragraphs, paragraph headings, bullet points, etc.;

  list the essential data. You may want to use tables, graphs and figures.

Use a consistent system of display throughout. Numbered paragraphs might be 1, 2, 3, or 1.1, 1.2, 1.3, etc.

Using effective "signposting" in this way will help the reader pick out elements of the report and will ensure the whole document is easy to follow.

Conclusions

Remember, the purpose of a report is to provide findings and draw conclusions from those findings. This section is vital in a report and allows the key arguments and findings of the report to be drawn together and put into context.

Conclusions need to:

 refer to the purpose of the report;

 state the main points arising in the report;

✓ be brief and concise.

Recommendations

Any recommendations you make must be presented clearly and follow logically from the conclusions.

This section might, for example, suggest a preferred option from several that were under consideration, make new proposals or recommend further research or investigation.

A Report

For the Legal Department of Doncaster Borough Council

on

Trees Subject to Tree Preservation Orders in the Borough

Written by
Teresa Green

15 February 2009

It is sensible to include on this front page a CONTENTS SECTION. For instance

The Report's Content

Terms of reference

Report on "Trees Subject to Tree Preservation Orders in the Borough" for the Legal Department of Doncaster Borough Council.

Title

Trees Subject to Tree Preservation Orders in the Borough

Findings

The Report was requested by the Legal Department of Doncaster Borough Council (the person[s], or Department) and gives details on:

Trees in domestic properties

Trees in the Borough's Parks

Trees in streets.

This is the section where you write about each part of the report in detail. For each topic use a heading, and possibly sub-headings, to emphasise the different parts of the topic. For instance:

Trees in domestic properties

The addresses of the properties where Tree Preservation Orders are in force

then include the necessary information.

The type of trees involved

then include the necessary information.

Conclusions

The purpose of the report was to ....

As can be seen from the "Findings", the Borough has a total of 235 trees subject to a Tree Preservation Order and the locations are set out in the map on page xx. (In this section you are describing the purpose and outcomes of the report.)

Recommendations

Describe the recommendations, making use of paragraphs, paragraph headings, bullet points, underlined headings, etc.

Writing a CV (Curriculum Vitae) and a Covering Letter

A CV (Curriculum Vitae) is a document that gives a brief account of someone's:

 education;

 qualifications;

 experience; and

is written by a job applicant to give information to a prospective employer (someone to whom the applicant is applying for a job).

It is important to state facts, that is not to tell lies, and to give positive information.

An example of how you might set out your CV and the information you should include is shown on *page 120*.

You must take care with spelling, grammar and punctuation and, if you are not presenting a typewritten CV, you must make sure your writing is clear. It is best to use black ink because the CV may be photocopied by the employer and black ink copies more successfully than any other colour.

Divide the information into sections, each under separate headings. Some are a must, whilst others are only useful if they are relevant to you.

See the suggested headings and layout on *page 120*.

Sample Layout for a CV

PERSONAL DETAILS	
Name	*Include your full name(s).*
Address	*Ideally put each line of your address on a separate line. Don't forget your **post code**.*
Telephone no.	*Include the area code if quoting a landline number.*
Date of birth/age	*Expressed as 8th March 1986 rather than 8/3/86.*
	Aged 23.
Nationality	*You might decide not to include this information.*
EDUCATION	
Last school attended and qualifications gained	*1999 – 2004 (name of school)*
	***List only the passes – be proud of your achievements**.*

2004 – GCSEs:

English Language	*Grade B*
Mathematics	*Grade C*

Key Skills:

Application of Number	*Level 2*
Communication	*Level 2*
ICT	*Level 1*

etc., etc., etc.

College attended and qualifications gained	*2004 – 2005 (name of college)*
Non-academic achievements	*Passing your driving test*
	Duke of Edinburgh Award
	etc., etc.
Work experience	*Name of firm(s), dates, job title, responsibilities*
Leisure interests (hobbies)	
Referees	*Include two people's names and addresses if possible – **however, check with them first that they agree to give you a reference**.*

Date (mm/yyyy). **You will need to know when your CV was written because you will be gaining additional qualifications and experience all the time and will want to update it for most job applications.**

Covering Letter to Accompany a CV

In this section you will learn how to:

▶ write clearly and coherently including an appropriate level of detail (W1.1)

▶ present information in a logical sequence (W1.2)

▶ use language, format and structure suitable for purpose and audience (W1.3)

▶ ensure written work includes accurate grammar, punctuation and spelling and that meaning is clear (W1.5)

Every time that you send out your CV you will need to send out a cover letter with it, whether you are sending your CV in response to an advertisement or direct to an employer.

A cover letter needs to say a lot more than just: 'Here is my CV!', which is all some people seem to think a cover letter should say.

It needs to tell the person why you are writing to them and outline why you are the ideal candidate for the job. You need to pick out the highlights from your CV that are relevant to the specific application, because most jobs you apply for will require a slightly different emphasis of your skills, qualifications and experience.

When employers receive hundreds of applications for one job it is important to get them to read and consider **your** CV. It is important to show them you have style and are just what they are looking for. A covering letter, clipped neatly to your CV, begins to get you noticed for the **right** reasons.

Points to Remember

✓ Use good quality, plain A4 paper.

✓ Use a fountain pen or a good quality ballpoint – it is acceptable to type your covering letter, but be sure, like on your CV, that spelling, grammar and punctuation is 100% accurate.

✓ Use black ink.

✓ If writing by hand, keep your lines straight – but do not use lined paper.

✓ Use neat and legible handwriting.

✓ Keep a copy of your CV and accompanying letter clipped together.

✓ Use the correct name and address, and the title of the person receiving the letter if you know it.

✓ Use a matching salutation and complimentary close.

12 Hospital Fields
York
YO1 5FW

30 November 2009

Miss M Stubbs
Personnel Manager
Fotherington and Crampton Store plc
2 Coppergate
YORK YO1 1FP

Dear Miss Stubbs

Your vacancy for a junior administrator

The Yorkshire Post 14 November 2009

I have read your advertisement for a junior administrator and I am keen to apply. Please find enclosed my CV with details of referees who have agreed they may be contacted on my behalf.

This would seem an ideal opportunity to combine my interest in computers and my interest in a retailing career, and I believe that I have the qualities and qualifications which your advertisement describes.

I am 17 years of age, I care about my appearance and I am enthusiastic and work well as a team member. Additionally, I have a computer and have done some introductory programming. I am ambitious and enjoy using my initiative and taking responsibility when given the opportunity.

I leave college on 21 November and I would be available to start work immediately afterwards. If you wish to interview me, I would be pleased to attend any day after 4pm or on a Saturday. After I leave college, I would be available for interview at any time.

I hope you will consider me as a candidate for the post.

Yours sincerely

Angelina Santos

Angelina Santos

Enc

The purpose of this letter is to add information that it is not normally possible to include on a CV because the headings can be somewhat limiting.

Another purpose is to try further to convince the reader that the writer is ideal for the job in question. Remember your CV or letter of application should get you invited for an interview. No good if it goes into the bin, you won't get your interview then.

Let's look at what Angelina wanted to add to support the facts on her CV:

1   What has Angelina made clear by including a heading to her letter?

        The reader can see immediately the post applied for. This is important information for the reader because there might not be just one job being advertised at a time, especially when the company is large.

        Angelina has included information about where she saw the post advertised. It is not strictly necessary that this information be included, but it does help a firm to decide which source of advertising was best for them so they can use that source in the future. Some firms do ask you to say where you saw the advertisement so it's a good idea to include it in your accompanying letter.

2   The first paragraph is a good opening and indicates a CV is included.

3   In the second paragraph Angelina is reinforcing the fact that she is interested in the job advertised and giving reasons why she thinks she should be considered.

4   Why do you think she has written the third paragraph?

        She's anxious to include some details that she thinks she will show her experience and interest as being suitable for the job and show her as someone who is ambitious and interested in working hard.

5   The fourth paragraph contains information that someone planning to interview Angelina will be pleased to have. By including this information, Angelina has made sure the reader knows when she will be available to start work (if she was appointed) and when she will be available for an interview (which she very clearly hopes she will get).

6   Her final paragraph reinforces how keen she is to be interviewed for the job.

I think the result of this letter is likely to lead to her being invited for the next step of the job application process.

All she needs to do now is read the Interview Tips on the following page and hopefully she'll get the job.

Interview Tips

Your job application form or your CV and covering letter impressed the prospective employer and you have been invited to attend an interview.

Study the following advice.

Arriving

Arrive early for your interview. To make sure you do this, carefully research public transport times/car parking arrangements. Know how long it will take you to walk to the employer's premises from the station, bus stop, car park, etc.

How to Dress

Dress smartly and appropriately — forget about being the height of fashion for the day, and don't overload the jewellery.

Walking into the Interview Room

When called in to your interview, walk confidently into the room.

It is usual to shake hands with the interviewer(s). A firm handshake is important.

Be Friendly

You should always maintain eye contact with the interviewer(s), especially with the person asking the question and with anyone to whom you are directing an answer.

Keep a friendly smile on your face to show your enthusiasm.

Sit up Straight

Sit up straight in the chair — don't slouch.

When you are nervous it is sometimes difficult to know what to do with your hands. When sitting, fold them on your lap and keep them still.

Speak Clearly

Speak clearly and slowly. When you are nervous there is a tendency to rush your words. Slow down.

Avoid slang terms and poor grammar, such as "like", "basically", "actually", "absolutely", "er", "no problem", "obviously".

Listening to and Answering Questions

Concentrate carefully on the questions you are asked and make sure you understand the question before you answer it.

If you don't fully understand a question, ask for it to be repeated.

Answer the question then stop talking. Don't go on and on and on with your answer.

You are allowed to think before you answer. However, don't spend too much time thinking.

Remember to direct your answer to the person who asked the question. If there are other people present, glance at them from time to time to include them in what you are saying.

Think in Advance

If you have done your research into the job description and the company well, you should be able to anticipate some of the questions you will be asked. Prepare for these before your interview and know what you will say.

Promote your Positive Achievements

Be honest about your weaknesses but positive about your achievements and strengths.

At the End of the Interview

Stand up and shake hands again, thanking the interviewer(s) for their time.

Walk confidently out of the room.

Some Likely Interview Questions

Think about your responses to the following commonly asked interview questions:

- Tell me about yourself.

- What are your greatest strengths and weaknesses?

- Why do you want to work for us?

- What kind of salary are you looking for?

- What do you know about our company?

- Why should we employ you?

- Where do you see yourself in five years time?

- Do you mind working long hours?

- Tell me what you like best about your present job, and why.

- Tell me what you like least about your present job, and why.

- Tell me about when you have taken any responsibility.

- How do you feel about gaining further qualifications?

Would You Like to Ask Any Questions?

When the interviewer has asked all the questions she/he wishes, you are likely to be asked if you wish to ask any questions. Prepare a few questions in advance.

Of course, your questions depend on what was covered during the interview, but think about the following as possible questions:

- Are there opportunities for progression/promotion?

- Would it be possible for me to go to college to gain further qualifications?

- Would I be expected to wear a uniform?

- Would it be possible to see where I would be working?

Finally, you can ask those all-important questions:

- What is the holiday entitlement?

- What is the salary?

Don't ask the last two questions first – whilst you want to know these things, if the interview has not already given you this information, ask other questions first. You don't want the interviewer to think your only concerns are holidays and money!

125

Taking Part in a Formal, or an Informal Discussion

What is the *purpose* of a discussion? It is an opportunity to share and exchange ideas and put forward arguments for and against a topic or idea.

Spend a few moments thinking of the roles you might take in a discussion.

Your role will vary in each discussion. You could be the person who is **encouraging** others to do something, or hoping to change their ideas; your role could be to **support** someone else's ideas or opinions. In any discussion it's important to show you are listening to the contribution of the other people involved.

You must expect to have to prepare for your discussion. This might involve making notes of the things you intend to say, such as your main ideas or arguments. You might have to do some research on a subject you don't know a lot about, or even research a subject that is new to you. This is where your research and reading skills will be important, together with your ability to write a range of documents for different audiences – some who understand the topic, others who know nothing about it.

Being Confident in a Discussion

You must think through your ideas and feelings before you begin. Preparing what you will say, and how you will say it, is the key to being confident.

Your Discussion Checklist

- ✓ Make sure you understand what is to be the topic of the discussion, and know what is expected of you in the discussion.

- ✓ Jot down your immediate thoughts, ideas and opinions.

- ✓ Conduct your research to give you a wider knowledge of the topic.

- ✓ Make notes from your research of the new ideas you have found useful, or extra information that will support your existing thoughts and ideas.

- ✓ Think about what you will say on the topic. You will usually favour one view, but should be aware that the other people might have different views, so you will need to think what you might say about these different views.

- ✓ Organise your ideas so they follow a logical order. This is especially important when you are planning a telephone call. Before making the call make a note of the reason for your call and the main things you need to say.

- ✓ Make notes of what you will say. Try to keep these mainly to headings so they are easy to *refer to* in the discussion. If you have done your research well, you will *know* your topic and be sufficiently confident to talk around the headings you have made. You will lose the others in the discussion if you read from your notes.

When you are talking, maintain eye contact with the others present and speak clearly (this usually means slowly).

Speaking slowly means you give yourself time to think and organise what you say and can think about your responses to questions the others may ask.

How to Show you are Listening

When you are in an encouraging or supporting role, you will mainly be listening to what others say. *Show* you are listening by looking at the person speaking, perhaps occasionally smiling or nodding. Make notes if you have to, in order to help you remember their main ideas, arguments or opinions.

Ask questions. Be polite and don't interrupt the person speaking. You are expected to act **reasonably**, which means politely, showing respect for the feelings and values of others.

As we have decided a discussion is a sharing of ideas, try to make sure *everyone* contributes. Whilst it is not very nice to put someone "on the spot" by asking directly "Martha, what are your ideas?" – you wouldn't like it said to you! – you can help Martha to contribute. Say something like "That's a good point, but we haven't heard Martha's ideas yet, let's give her a chance." This is kinder and suggests her contribution is equally valuable.

Finally, *the aim* of a discussion is usually to reach an agreement about a topic and decide what to do next. Don't let the discussion go round in circles. Keep reminding everyone of the purpose (e.g. to decide responsibilities for organising the keep fit class, to decide on the arguments for and against teenage smoking and related health damage, etc.). Summarise what has been said/agreed, then move on to the next part of the discussion.

At the end of the discussion, summarise what has been said or decided and make sure everyone has the opportunity to agree.

> **REMEMBER: You don't have to agree with the opinions of others, but this does not give you the right to dismiss what others say. Show people respect at all times.**

SECTION 3

PRACTISING READING, WRITING, SPEAKING AND LISTENING SKILLS

The Three Sections of Functional Skills English

There are **three** sections to the Functional Skills English Level 1 Standards, each of which focuses on a different aspect of communicating.

The focuses are:

Speaking and Listening (SL)

Reading (R)

Writing (W)

As you can see from the diagram below, each focus is linked to either one, or both, of the other two.

Each focus contains information on what has to be achieved by a successful candidate. Your skills will be tested, some of them in an examination (*see page 132*).

The purpose of this section of the book is to offer a range of tasks, linked to various employment sectors, that will help you acquire and practise the skills so you become competent and confident. This competence and confidence will help you pass the examination and also to become a student and an employee who can work independently and effectively.

Functional English: Purposeful Activities

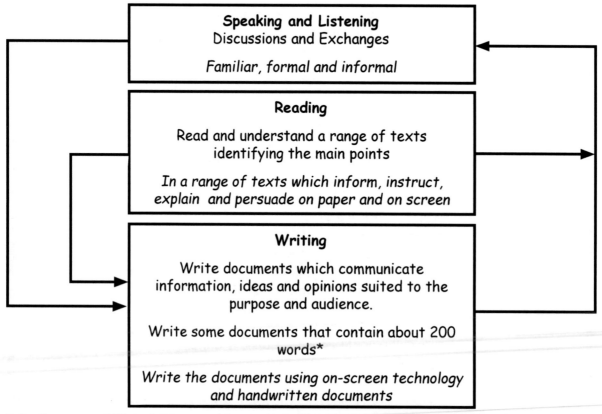

Speaking and Listening
Discussions and Exchanges

Familiar, formal and informal

Reading

Read and understand a range of texts identifying the main points

In a range of texts which inform, instruct, explain and persuade on paper and on screen

Writing

Write documents which communicate information, ideas and opinions suited to the purpose and audience.

Write some documents that contain about 200 words*

Write the documents using on-screen technology and handwritten documents

* For the purpose of this book it is assumed the standards will eventually suggest the need to write at least one document of about 200 words. Not all documents to be written need to be this length.

No focus stands by itself: each focus is linked to another

- A document is never read and summarised without its content forming part of the written document, or the topic of a discussion/exchange.
- In order to prepare for a discussion/exchange (speaking and listening), there might be the need for some research, which involves reading documents, then notes being written to help with the discussion/exchange.
- **As a result of a discussion/exchange there can be the need to write a document or to** conduct further research and **read** other documents.
- After a discussion/exchange there is usually an opportunity to **listen** to questions or comments from the other person(s) taking part in the discussion/exchange.

Employment sectors represented by tasks in this section:

Sector of employment	Company name
Chid Care	Jack and Jill Children's Nursery
Construction Industry	
Building	Another Brick in the Wall
Joinery	Plane Designs
Painting and Decorating	Painted Ladies
Plumbing	Primary Plumbing
Entertainment	Gigs Galore
Hairdressing	Snippers Hair and Beauty Salon
Horticulture	All Dug Up
Hospitality Industry	1925 Restaurant
	Palm Trees Hotel
Journalism	Barley Wynd Bugle
	Polkerith Post
Local Government	Larchfield Village Council
Motor Trade	Vroom Vroom
Retail	Home Comforts 'R' Us
	Marginal Matters
Travel	Isaac Newton Airport
	Sunny Destinations Travel
Utility Company	Lustram Water Company Ltd

The range of tasks are designed to provide you with practice for all the Functional English Level 1 content. As you need to become competent in each of the required areas in Functional English Level 1, your tutor will probably want you to practise tasks from more than just the employment sector in which you are involved, or are interested in following.

Additionally, when you are involved in work for a variety of sectors, you might find it easier to choose a pathway for employment, and be interested in having work experience in an area you had not previously considered.

Another reason for practising work from a variety of employment sectors is because the examination which you will do to prove your competence in Functional English Level 1, will be on a general topic, or topics, and not necessarily linked to a specific employment sector. Because of this, you need to be able to understand and produce documents on a wide range of subjects.

The type of documents and tasks in this book include:

- Completing forms
- Writing memos
- Interpreting information in tables and charts
- Reading maps
- Writing business letters
- Writing personal letters
- Writing advertisements
- Writing emails
- Writing faxes
- Researching subjects
- Taking part in a discussion
- Taking part in telephone calls

In each task you complete, you must pay attention to using correct grammar, spelling and punctuation, and for those tasks that you handwrite, your writing must be clear and the documents neat and tidy.

Task 1: Painted Ladies — An Estimate For A Customer

Student Information	REMEMBER
In this task you will read instructions then complete an estimate. Ask your Tutor for a copy of the **Painted Ladies** estimate.	Your form must be completed neatly and contain accurate information. Take care with handwriting and spelling. Read the headings on the estimate so you are sure which information is needed. See *"Completing Forms and Job Application Forms"* on page 75. Make sure you express the dates as dd/mm/yyyy in order to be clear and avoid confusion.

Reading Information and Completing an Estimate

Scenario

Painted Ladies is a painting and decorating firm run by two ladies and today you are preparing an estimate.

Activities

One of the partners, Pamela Crimson, has been to see a potential customer. She has now asked you to prepare an estimate related to some inside painting work.

1   Look at the blank estimate form shown in **Appendix 1** so you know what information is needed.

2   Study the information shown in **Appendix 2** and transfer the information onto the blank estimate which your tutor will give you.

3   Sign the form on behalf of Pamela (you can sign her name). Date the estimate **today**.

Take care with spelling and your handwriting and make sure what you write is correct and that everything you include is in the correct place.

PAINTED LADIES DECORATORS
Primrose Lane, Blanchland,
Northumberland
NB31 2PL

01595 316161

Pamela Crimson & Mia Scarlet

ESTIMATE

Customer's Name ....

Customer's Address ....

Job Description	Estimated time of job	Estimate £
AVAILABLE START DATE(S)		

Signed .... Date .... 200...

Appendix 2

The Customer's Name is Mrs P Coates

The Customer's Address is 72 Willow Way, Morpeth, Northumberland   NB11 6HX

The Job Description is as follows :

Painting 1 coat of undercoat (white) and 1 coat of "Supershine" bright white gloss to both sides of 18 doors and door frames.

The job will take 4 days and the cost is £323.00

There are two available start dates — the first Monday and the second Tuesday of next month. (Put in the appropriate dates by using a calendar or diary to find the correct dates.)

The estimate is dated **today** and you can sign it on behalf Pamela Crimson.

Task 2: Isaac Newton Airport, Your Town — Bus Timetables

Student Information	REMEMBER
In this task you will read timetables then complete an email to a friend. Ask your Tutor for a copy of the **email** document.	Write the information in the email clearly and with neat handwriting. See *"Reading and Understanding Information Displayed in Tables"* on page 87 Look at the headings to make sure which information needs to be included and take care to include the information in the correct place.

Interpreting Timetables and Completing an Email

Scenario

Your friend is flying into your local airport to spend a holiday with you and you have to offer advice on getting from the airport to the town/city centre.

Activities

Your friend will be arriving on Wednesday of next week and the aeroplane is scheduled to land at 10:35. You have to advise how she/he can get from the **Isaac Newton Airport** to the town/city centre where you will be waiting. She/he is flying by Wings Airline.

1   Study the timetables shown in **Appendix 1** and decide which Aero-bus **and** public transport would be appropriate for your friend. Bear in mind that if the flight is on time it will take approximately 30 minutes for your friend to get out of the airport after landing.

2   Make a note of the times which you think are the most suitable, for each method of transport, and add to this any other important information on the email document your tutor gave you.

      A sample of the email that you have to compete is shown in **Appendix 2**.

Appendix 1

AERO-BUS TIMETABLE

The Aero-bus provides transport from the Airport into the town/city centre, which is a distance of 17 miles.

It is free for British Airways passengers on presentation of your aeroplane ticket/ boarding card. For all other passengers the **single** journey cost is £8.00.

The bus stop is located beside the exit from the baggage reclaim hall on the ground floor outside the passenger terminal.

AERO-BUS TIMETABLE*

ISAAC NEWTON AIRPORT			
Departure Town/City Centre	Arrival Airport	Departure Airport	Arrival Town/City Centre
08:00	08:30	09:30	10:00
10:15	10:45	11:30	12:00
12:15	12:45	14:15	15:45
15:00	15:30	16:00	16:30
17:00	17:30	18:00	18:30
19:15	19:45	20:00	20:30
21:00	21:30	22:30	23:00

Appendix 1 continued

BUS TIMETABLE

The stop for the public bus service can be found at the Airport exit signposted "Town/City Centre". The journey into the town/city centre takes about 1 hour and costs £3.85.

BUS TIMETABLE* (No. 115 and 116)

ISAAC NEWTON AIRPORT			
Departure Town/City Centre	Arrival Airport	Departure Airport	Arrival Town/City Centre
116		115	
07:05	08:05	07:15	08:15
08:45	09:45	08:45	09:45
10:20	11:20	09:20	10:20
12:00	13:00	10:15	11:15
13:45	14:45	11:30	12:30
14:30	15:30	13:00	14:00
15:40	16:40	14:15	15:15
16:00	17:00	15:00	16:00
17:45	18:45	16:30	17:30
19:30	20:30	17:50	18:50
21:00	22:00	19:45	20:45
21:30	22:30	21:15	22:15

* times are **daily**

Appendix 2

To: myfriend@starburts.co.uk
Cc:
Bcc:
Subject: Getting from Isaac Newton airport to the town/city

Tahoma

Hello: I'm pleased you are arriving next Wednesday and hope your plane is on time. I am sorry I can't meet you at the airport but I've looked into **bus** and **aero-bus** times and can tell you the times which I think will be most suitable for you. These are:

Method of Transport   1   2   Cost   1   2

Departure time   1   2

Location of transport   1   2

The transport will drop you at the Town Hall and I will be waiting for you if you email me to say what time you will be arriving there. I'm looking forward to seeing you and have a busy 5 days planned for us, including going to a local football match. I have a spare blue and white scarf if you don't have one!!

Looking forward to next week.

Best wishes

Task 3: Jack and Jill Children's Nursery — Completing an Advertisement

Student Information	REMEMBER
In this task you will read instructions and complete an advertisement.	Use a dictionary for any words you are not certain of.
Ask your tutor for a copy of the **Advertisement** sheet.	An adjective is a word that describes something — like black, sweet, orderly and loud.

Reading Text and Completing an Advertisement

Scenario

The two Nursery Managers are planning to place an advertisement in the local newspaper to encourage new clients.

Activities

The Nursery Managers are Ruth Swanage and Katrina Paxton. Ruth has put together an advertisement, in draft, that she wants you to amend for her.

Ask your tutor for a copy of the advertisement.

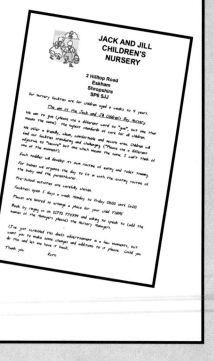

1   Study the draft advertisement, and Ruth's notes, shown in **Appendix 1**, and make the changes that Ruth requests.

     Make sure your handwriting is neat and can be read.

JACK AND JILL CHILDREN'S NURSERY

**2 Hilltop Road
Eskham
Shropshire
SP6 5JJ**

Our nursery facilities are for children aged 6 weeks to 4 years.

<u>The aim of the Jack and Jill Children's Day Nursery</u>

We aim to give (please use a different word to "give", but one that means the same) the highest standards of care for all children.

We offer a friendly, clean, comfortable and secure area. Children will find our facilities stimulating and challenging. ("Please use a different adjective to "secure" but one which means the same. I can't think of one at the moment).

Each toddler will develop its own routine of eating and toilet training.

For babies we organise the day to fit in with the existing routine of the baby and the parent/carer.

Pre-School activities are carefully chosen.

Facilities: open 5 days a week Monday to Friday 08:00 until 16:00

Places are limited so arrange a place for your child TODAY

Book by ringing us on 01772 778334 and asking to speak to (add the names of the Managers please) the Nursery Managers.

(I've just scribbled this draft advertisement in a few moments, but want you to make some changes and additions to it please. Could you do this and let me have it back?

Thank you   Ruth

Task 4: Painted Ladies — Organising a Job Rota

Student Information	REMEMBER
In this task you will read instructions and display a schedule of work on a Job Rota form.	Read the information carefully so you understand what you have to do.
	Study the column headings so you know which information to include and where it belongs.
Ask your tutor for two blank **Job Rota** forms.	See "Completing Forms and Job Application Forms" on page 75.
	Make sure your writing is clear and neat and all spelling is correct.
	Make sure what you write is accurate.
	When arranging text in **date order** follow the calendar, i.e. 3rd March would come on the list before 18th March.

Reading Information and Completing a Form

Scenario

You work for the decorating firm called **Painted Ladies** and today must put together a work schedule for the jobs already booked for next month.

Activities

Pamela Crimson and Mia Scarlet have been making notes about their bookings for next month. These are shown in **Appendix 1**.

1   Study the information in **Appendix 1** which details the decorating jobs confirmed for next month.

2   Arrange the jobs, **in date order**, on the Job Rota forms which your tutor will give you. An example of the Job Rota Form is shown in **Appendix 2**.

> NOTE: you have the task of allocating jobs to the two partners, only one partner is needed on each job.

12th - 14th (3 days) Hall and Staircase papering and painting Dr and Mrs P Sinclair 6 Piper Court, Slaley

5th - 8th (4 days)

Stripping existing paper, papering and painting bungalow's hall

Professor D Lacey, Mill Cottage, Peartree Lane, Whitley Chapel

21st and 22nd Painting bathroom and WC for Miss L Hope

116 Cathryn Court, Hunstanworth

2nd and 3rd Mr and Mrs A Saltman

Papering bedroom

4 Northumberland Avenue,

Whitley Chapel

4th and 5th - Painting kitchen walls and ceiling Miss J Oswald, Flat 4, Bernadette House, Morpeth

11th and 12th painting inside of conservatory for Mrs L Horowich, 3 Chestnut Grove, Ruffside

Outside painting of bungalow 25th - 28th (4 days) Mr and Mrs N Silverton, 9 Ashville Avenue, Rookhope

PAINTED LADIES JOB ROTA
FOR THE MONTH OF

Job Description	Dates Start	Finish	No. of days	Partner	Customer's Name	Customer's Address

Task 5: All Dug Up Nursery — Organising a Newspaper Competition

Student Information	REMEMBER
In this task you will read an article for a newspaper and answer some questions.	Read the information carefully, possibly two or three times. Answer the questions then check your answers carefully.

Reading an Article and Answering Questions

Scenario

Allan Dugworth is the owner of a gardening business called **All Dug Up**. Allan also writes a gardening column for the local evening newspaper called the Barley Wynd Bugle. Today he is writing his weekly gardening competition for the newspaper.

Activities

Allan Dugworth has written the gardening competition that will appear in next week's newspaper on Monday evening. As usual, he asks you to check it by reading it and answering the questions.

1   Read the Article shown in **Appendix 1**.

2   Make a note of the answers to each of the five questions.

3   Hand your answers to your tutor and when they are returned to you keep them safely as you will need to refer to them in **Task 7**.

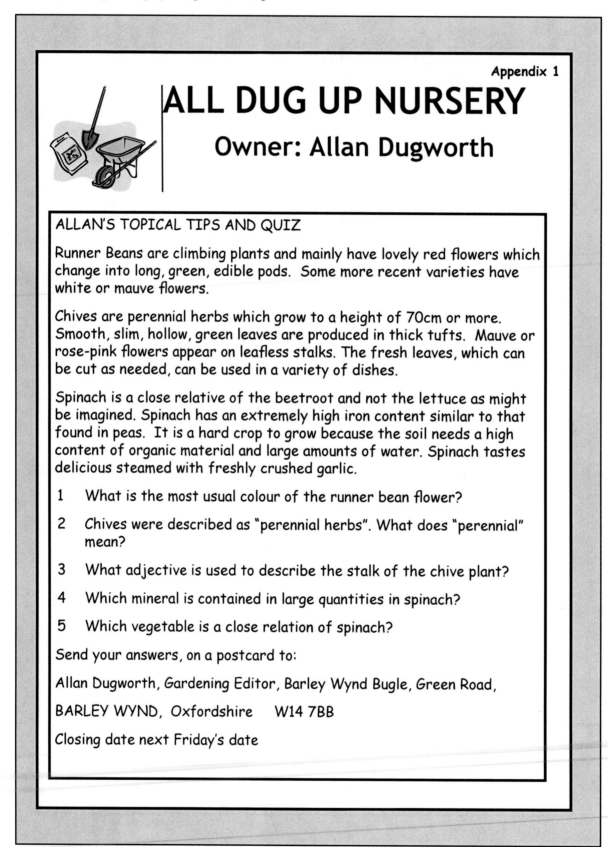

ALL DUG UP NURSERY
Owner: Allan Dugworth

ALLAN'S TOPICAL TIPS AND QUIZ

Runner Beans are climbing plants and mainly have lovely red flowers which change into long, green, edible pods. Some more recent varieties have white or mauve flowers.

Chives are perennial herbs which grow to a height of 70cm or more. Smooth, slim, hollow, green leaves are produced in thick tufts. Mauve or rose-pink flowers appear on leafless stalks. The fresh leaves, which can be cut as needed, can be used in a variety of dishes.

Spinach is a close relative of the beetroot and not the lettuce as might be imagined. Spinach has an extremely high iron content similar to that found in peas. It is a hard crop to grow because the soil needs a high content of organic material and large amounts of water. Spinach tastes delicious steamed with freshly crushed garlic.

1   What is the most usual colour of the runner bean flower?

2   Chives were described as "perennial herbs". What does "perennial" mean?

3   What adjective is used to describe the stalk of the chive plant?

4   Which mineral is contained in large quantities in spinach?

5   Which vegetable is a close relation of spinach?

Send your answers, on a postcard to:

Allan Dugworth, Gardening Editor, Barley Wynd Bugle, Green Road,

BARLEY WYND, Oxfordshire   W14 7BB

Closing date next Friday's date

Task 6: Barley Wynd Bugle Newspaper — The Gardening Competition

Student Information

In this task you will read information then write a memo.

Ask your tutor for a blank **Barley Wynd Bugle** memo sheet, **and** the **Competition Sheet** written by Allan Dugworth.

REMEMBER

Your memo should be brief and you must sign it.

Add the title of the persons sending and receiving the Memo, as well as their names.

See *"Writing and Setting Out Memos"* on page 80.

Writing a Memo

Scenario

You work in the Gardening section of the Barley Wynd Bugle evening newspaper and have to write a memo to arrange for competition details to be included in next Monday's paper.

Activities

1   Read the Memo you have received from Lavender Bush the Gardening Editor. This is shown in **Appendix 1**.

2   Do as Lavender asks, sending and signing the memo from yourself.

3   Staple your Memo to the Competition Sheet and hand both documents to your tutor.

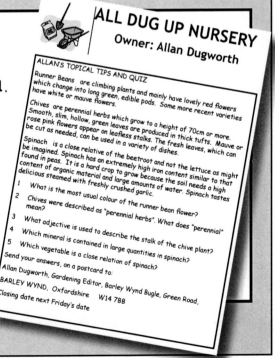

ALL DUG UP NURSERY
Owner: Allan Dugworth

ALLAN'S TOPICAL TIPS AND QUIZ

Runner Beans are climbing plants and mainly have lovely red flowers which change into long green, edible pods. Some more recent varieties have white or mauve flowers.

Chives are perennial herbs which grow to a height of 70cm or more. Smooth, slim, hollow, green leaves are produced in thick tufts. Mauve or rose pink flowers appear on leafless stalks. The fresh leaves, which can be cut as needed, can be used in a variety of dishes.

Spinach is a close relative of the beetroot and not the lettuce as might be imagined. Spinach has an extremely high iron content similar to that found in peas. It is a hard crop to grow because the soil needs a high content of organic material and large amounts of water. Spinach tastes delicious steamed with freshly crushed garlic.

1   What is the most usual colour of the runner bean flower?

2   Chives were described as "perennial herbs". What does "perennial" mean?

3   What adjective is used to describe the stalk of the chive plant?

4   Which mineral is contained in large quantities in spinach?

5   Which vegetable is a close relation of spinach?

Send your answers, on a postcard to:

Allan Dugworth, Gardening Editor, Barley Wynd Bugle, Green Road, BARLEY WYND, Oxfordshire   W14 7BB

Closing date next Friday's date

MEMORANDUM

To   *Student's name*

Date: *Yesterday's date*

From: Lavender Bush,
        Gardening Editor

Re: Next week's gardening competition
        from Allan Dugworth

I've received the attached competition from Allan Dugworth which I agree will appear in Monday's paper.

Please could you send a Memo to the Deputy Editor, Troy Stanniviz, saying you are enclosing next week's gardening competition which I have approved.

Say that this time the competition takes up more space than usual so we will need a half page spread.

Thank you.

Lavender

Att

Task 7: Barley Wynd Bugle — The Competition Winner

Student Information	Remember
In this task you will check competition entries with the work you did in **Task 5**, then write a Memo naming the competition winner.	Your Memo should be brief and you must sign it.
	See *"Writing and Setting Out Memos"* on page 80.
	See *"Reading and Understanding Information Displayed in Tables"* on page 87.
Ask your tutor for a blank **Barley Wynd Bugle** memo sheet.	

Interpreting Information and Writing a Memo

Scenario

Allan Dugworth must now check the answers to the competition he wrote and select a winner.

Activities

Lavender Bush, the Gardening Editor, has handed to Allan Dugworth a summary of the competition entries which she thinks contain the correct answers to Allan's competition. You have to select the person who has answered all five questions correctly, and then write a memo to Lavender giving the winner's details.

The memo will be from Allan Dugworth and he must sign it, so when it has been written, sign his name.

1   Read the details contained in **Appendix 1**.

2   Check the answers against the **correct** answers which you noted in **Task 5**.

3   Select the winning entry and write a memo to Lavender Bush giving her this information. Head the Memo **Gardening Competition Winner**.

4   Mention that the winner will receive a £50 voucher to spend in All Dug Up Nursery.

SUMMARY OF COMPETITION ENTRIES WITH THE MOST CORRECT ANSWERS

Entrants' Names	Entrants' Addressed	Entrants' Answers	
The Reverend K Harper	The Rectory The Green Barley Wynd BW3 7BH	1 2 3 4 5	white temporary leafless iron peas
Miss J Culpepper	Ashtree Cottage The Green Barley Wynd BW3 7BG	1 2 3 4 5	red occasional leafless iron beetroot
Mr Rupert Brownlee	6 Ashville Court Grainger Close Appletreewick Village BW3 9BC	1 2 3 4 5	white or purple lasting pink iron beetroot
Mrs J Lynd	11 Nursery Fields Appletreewick Village BW8 3VF	1 2 3 4 5	red continuing leafless iron garlic
Dr L Cuthbert	Surgery House 9 Chester Road Barley Wynd BW3 1KM	1 2 3 4 5	red continuing leafless iron beetroot
Mrs E Upton	83 Copper Crescent Barley Wynd BW3 6DW	1 2 3 4 5	red constant thick iron beetroot

Task 8: Lustram Water Company — Maintaining the Water Pipes

Student Information	REMEMBER
In this task you will read information and display extracted information in a table.	Read the information in the table carefully. *See "Reading and Understanding Information Displayed in Tables" on page 87.* Your handwriting must be neat and legible. Check to make sure you include all the information which is required. When arranging text in **date order** follow the calendar, i.e. 3rd March would come on the list before 18th March.

Interpreting, Extracting and Arranging Information

Scenario

You work in the offices of the Lustram Water Company. For the last three, and the next two months, it is renewing main water pipes in the Lustram area of central England.

Activities

You have to prepare details for an advertisement which will go in the local newspaper to advise householders of a planned interruption to their water supply.

1   Read the information shown in **Appendix 1** and make a note of the addresses of properties affected for **longer than three hours**.

2   Put the information you have extracted into a table using the following headings:

<u>Day</u>   <u>Date</u>   <u>Start time</u>   <u>End Time</u>   <u>Address</u>

Arrange the days and dates in date order and on <u>each</u> day arrange the addresses in alphabetical order.

3   Keep a copy of the table you produce as you will need this in **Task 14**.

LUSTRAM WATER COMPANY LTD
NOTIFICATION OF INTERRUPTION TO
HOUSEHOLD WATER SUPPLY FROM
(First Monday of Next Month)

Day and Date	Location	Times when the supply will be interrupted
Monday *first Monday's date*	1 — 14 Matilda Avenue	9am — 2pm
	High Street	8am — 10am
	Pilgrim Street	9am — 12 noon
	Henry Street	10am — 3pm
Tuesday *first Tuesday's date*	15 — 27 Matilda Avenue	9am — 2pm
	1 — 6 Pearl Avenue	8am — 11am
	1 — 8 Hyacinth Grove	10am — 3pm
	Rupert Street	10am — 3pm
	Highfield Farm	12 noon — 3pm
Wednesday *first Wednesday's date*	1 — 14 Pearl Avenue	8am — 12 noon
	9 — 20 Hyacinth Grove	10am — 2pm
	Hoyland Crescent	12 noon — 2pm
	Front Street	9am — 12 noon
	High Moor Farm	2pm — 4pm
Thursday *first Thursday's date*	Martindale Grove	9am — 1pm
	Carmichael Crescent	10am — 2pm
	Badgers' Green Farm	12 noon — 3pm
Friday *first Friday's date*	Conyers Lane	8am — 11am
	Simpkin Green	9am — 1pm
	Black Cat Inn	9am — 4pm
	East Farm	12 noon — 4pm

Lustram Water Company Ltd is undertaking essential renewal of mains water pipes in the Lustram area and notice is given that the water supply will be interrupted in the following properties on the dates and at the times, given in the table above.

If householders have any questions or concerns please telephone the Maintenance Hotline on 0800 456 229

08:00 – 20:00 Monday to Saturday

09:00 – 14:00 Sunday

Task 9: Home Comforts 'R' Us — A Furniture Sale

Student Information	REMEMBER
In this task you will read information and display extracted information in a table.	Read the instructions carefully so you understand what you have to do.
	See "Reading and Understanding Information Displayed in Tables" on page 87.
	Your handwriting must be neat and able to be read.
	Check to make sure you include all the information which is required.
	When arranging figures in **ascending order** arrange the list from lowest at the top to highest at the bottom, i.e. 297 to 445.

Interpreting, Extracting and Arranging Information

Scenario

Home Comforts 'R' Us is a furniture store and it is having a sale of three-piece suites. You will be organising advertising details.

Activities

The Store Manager, Marcus Larch, has asked you to prepare a list relating to the three-piece suites which will be offered in the sale beginning next month.

The suites included in the sale are listed in **Appendix 1**.

1   Produce a table with the information rearranged so that the **Sale Price** is in ascending numerical order. Include only the **Range Names**, the **Original Selling Price** and the **Sale Price** information. You can arrange these columns in any order.

> NOTE: use the table heading shown in Appendix 1.

Appendix 1

THREE-PIECE SUITE SALE DETAILS

Range Name	Available in the following colours	Sale Price	Original Selling Price
Calgary	Beige; Emperor Blue	£345	£700
Lisbon	Beige; Sea Blue	£420	£505
Vienna	Mid Brown; Apple Green	£400	£550
Prague	Deep Brown; Emperor Blue	£550	£650
Berlin	Gold; Apple Green	£500	£650
Dover	Rose; Beige	£560	£750
Warsaw	Mid Brown; Beige	£680	£850
Oslo	Apple Green	£665	£800
Rome	Gold; Mid Grey; Leaf Green	£695	£900
Madrid	Sea Blue	£675	£800

Task 10: Another Brick in the Wall — A Telephone Message

Student Information	REMEMBER
In this task you will read details of a message which has been received overnight on the company's answering machine, and leave details of the message for a colleague.	You need to make notes so that your telephone message is clear and includes only the relevant points. See "Using the Telephone and Making Telephone Calls" on page 104.

Reading Information and Placing a Call on a Telephone Answering Machine

Scenario

Another Brick in the Wall is a building company with building projects in various parts of the country. Today you receive a message about site meeting details.

Activities

The telephonist has written a word-for-word message that was left overnight for a member of staff. You have to select the important points and leave a message on that member of staff's answering machine.

1   Read the message that has been left — this is shown in **Appendix 1**.

2   Highlight the important points, leaving out any information which might be interesting but is not relevant.

3   Put your highlighted text into a logical order so it forms a telephone message you will leave on your colleague's answering machine.

4   With your tutor listening, make the "call" to Jasper Bennett's answering machine and leave the message you prepared in **Activity 3**.

5   Hand the notes you prepared in **Activity 3** to your tutor.

Appendix 1

Good evening, this is a message for Mr Jasper Bennett about his meeting at the Cooper Lane Site on Monday of next week.

The meeting has to take place at The Paddock site — as he knows that's only at the other end of Ashcombe village — because of the recent bad weather in Ashcombe Village which has caused some flooding of the Cooper Lane Site. This was unexpected rain for three days non-stop and we don't know why the site is flooded as it has not happened before. Don't think the flooding is too serious but it means we cannot get onto the site until it dries out, which the Site Manager says will be around Wednesday, Tuesday if we're lucky and get some decent dry weather.

Anyway we're meeting at The Paddock at 9.30 on Monday. The Cooper Lane Site Manager will be present — that's Tom Cowley — he's new to the job and has only been working on that Site for two weeks.

The hotel booking for Mr Bennett remains unchanged — that's a room in The Red Lion at Steeply Hill. Get Mr Bennett to ring me today at the office would you. I'll be there from 10:00 to 17:00.

Better tell Mr Bennett the hotel telephone number in case any problems occur with his travel arrangements and he will be late — they are holding the room until 6.30pm. Anyway it's 01886 2390011. My office telephone number is 01832 888309. The hotel's booked for Sunday evening.

If he can't ring me during office hours I suppose he'd better ring my mobile although I will be out at the theatre with some friends — a long-standing engagement which I don't want to cancel — from 7 until 11pm. The number is 07735 124708. Think that's all —. oh, no, tell Jasper I've booked a taxi for him from The Red Lion at 9.15am on Monday. He will probably arrange with the taxi driver when to take him back after the site meeting — that's up to him.

Sorry, forgot to say who this is — Tania Trent from Head Office. Thanks. Bye.

Task 11: Marginal Matters — Placing an Order

Student Information	REMEMBER
In this task you will complete an Order Form from information given to you. Ask your tutor for a blank **Marginal Matters** order form.	Read the instructions, and the headings on the form carefully so you understand what you have to do and which information to include. Your form must be completed neatly and contain accurate and relevant information. Correct spelling is important too. See "Completing Forms and Job Application Forms" on page 75.

Completing an Order Form

Scenario

You work in the office of one branch of **Marginal Matters**, a large national bookshop, and have to place an order for a book.

Activities

The Manager of the store — Iain Potts — has received the advertising flyer shown in **Appendix 1** and has decided to order 400 copies of the book. You have to complete the Order Form.

1   Read the advertising flyer (**Appendix 1**) and make sure you know the following:

   a)   the name of the new book and its author;

   b)   the ISBN number (the 13-digit number allocated to the book);

   c)   the cost of the book; and

   d)   the name and address of the company selling the book.

2   Complete the Marginal Matters Order Form.

3   You can sign the order. Please date it with today's date.

Appendix 1

COLWYN AND IRELAND PUBLISHING HOUSE
ANNOUNCE THE FORTHCOMING PUBLICATION OF

SWALLOWS FLY SOUTH

THE THIRD NOVEL

BY BEST-SELLING AUTHOR

VALENTINE EDENBRIDGE

HARDBACK EDITION (£11.99)

Set in Anglesey, **Swallows Fly South** tells the story of the Raphael family's boat-building business which runs into unexpected difficulties when a visitor to the island brings unwelcome news. The news sets in motion a train of events which threaten to uncover the family's secret which dates back more than a century.

The first novel by Valentine Edenbridge **THE RAINBOW SEEKER** Sold over 40,000 copies in the United Kingdom

ORDER "SWALLOWS FLY SOUTH" TODAY

ISBN 000-4181913-12-3

The second novel by Valentine Edenbridge **COLUMBINE HARVEST** Sold over 50,000 copies in the United Kingdom

Units 11-13 Falconbridge Way Old Trafford

MANCHESTER   M28 7JE

Task 12: Marginal Matters — Where's the Order?

Student Information	REMEMBER
In this task you will make a telephone call and write a memo. Ask your tutor for a blank **Marginal Matters** memo sheet.	Make notes before your telephone call so you are sure what you will say. *See "Using the Telephone and Making Telephone Calls" on page 104* Make notes of what is said during the telephone call because you will use some of this information in the memo you write. Speak clearly and make sure you give accurate information. End the call politely. *See "Writing and Setting Out Memos" on page 80.*

Making a Telephone Call and Writing a Memo

Scenario

You work for a branch of the national bookshop **Marginal Matters**. You ordered some books that have not arrived. Today you have to follow up this order.

Activities

The books you ordered in **Task 11** have not yet been received. Iain Potts, the store's Manager, wants you to ring Colwyn and Ireland to ask when you are likely to receive the books.

1.   With your tutor taking the role of an employee of the booksellers, Colwyn and Ireland, make the telephone call mentioning the following:

        a)   your name and your company's name;

        b)   what your call is about;

        c)   the **date** you placed your order;

        d)   the order **number**;

e)   the book title and the quantity you ordered.

Say you have not received the books yet and want to know when you can expect delivery.

2   Make a note of what you are told in the conversation so you can give Iain accurate information.

3   Write a memo to Iain giving him all the necessary information and facts.

Task 13: Snippers Hair and Beauty Salon — A Job Interview

Student Information	REMEMBER
In this task you will write a personal letter responding to one received which offers you a job interview.	A personal letter is written from someone's home address to either an individual person, or a company (as in this task). See *"Writing and Setting Out Personal Letters"* on page 108. Spelling, grammar and punctuation are important. Remember to sign the letter.

Writing a Personal Business Letter

Scenario

You have applied for a full-time job in a local hair and beauty salon and the owner has written to you offering you an interview. You are going to confirm you will attend the interview.

Activities

You have received the letter from **Snippers (Appendix 1)** and now will reply confirming you will attend the interview next week.

1   Write a letter in reply, using the heading **Interview for Post of Trainee Stylist**.

Note When you set out your letter you can use either "your" address shown on the letter from Snippers, **or** your own address.

2   Address the letter to Mr T Sampler and use a matching complimentary close.

3   Thank Mr Sampler for inviting you for interview (name the time and the **correct date**), and say you will be pleased to attend and that you will be bringing your certificates with you.

4   Sign the letter.

Appendix 1

SNIPPERS   HAIR   AND   BEAUTY   SALON

18   Steeple   Road   Altrincham   Cheshire   CW5   8BR   01511   343024

Letter dated yesterday

Student's name
3 Everton Dene
ALTRINCHAM
Cheshire
CW7 3LK

Dear *Student's first name*

POST OF TRAINEE STYLIST

Thank you for your letter and accompanying CV for the above-named, full-time post, which was advertised in the Sethcote Journal last week.

I am pleased to offer you an interview for the job, and would like you to attend on Thursday next week at 11am. Please bring with you any certificates which confirm the qualifications you have mentioned in your Curriculum Vitae.

Please confirm you are able to attend on this day and at the time stated.

I look forward to meeting you on Thursday.

Yours sincerely

Terry Sampler

Terry Sampler
Owner

Task 14: Lustram Water Company — Advertising The Water Interruption Details

Student Information	REMEMBER
In this task you will write a business letter.	A business letter is a formal document. *See "Writing and Setting Out Business Letters" on page 97.*
Ask your tutor for a blank **Lustram Water Company** letterheading.	*See "Useful Phrases for Business Letters" on page 100.*
	Make sure your letter contains the following :
	- the date it was written,
	- the title, name and address of the person who will receive the letter,
	- a salutation (Dear ?),
	- a complimentary close that matches the salutation,
	- the name of the person who wrote the letter.
	Be sure to sign the letter.

Writing a Business Letter

Scenario

You work in the offices of the Lustram Water Company and have to arrange for an advertisement to be placed in the local newspaper, The Lustram Post.

Activities

Following your work in **Task 8** you now have to write to the local newspaper sending them the table you prepared and arranging for an advertisement to be included next week. You will write and sign the letter.

1   Write a letter to Russell Webb, the Public Notices Manager of the Lustram Post whose address is Fleetwood House, Barnaby Road, Lustram, West Midlands, LM1 4DG. Ask him to insert the information contained in the table (say you are attaching the document) on Thursday and Friday of next week - quote the dates.

2   Ask for the account to be sent to the Accounts Manager of Lustram Water Company, Miss Erin Miller.

3 Use the salutation "Dear Mr Webb" and a matching complimentary close "Yours sincerely".

4 Attach a copy of your table to the letter you write and hand both pieces of work to your tutor.

Task 15: Personal Interest — Directing A Friend

Student Information	REMEMBER
In this task you will study a village map then write a personal letter to a friend.	See "Writing and Setting Out Personal Letters" on page 108. Spelling, grammar and punctuation are important. Remember to sign the letter.

Reading a Map and Writing a Personal Letter

Scenario

A friend is coming to stay with you for a weekend and you have to write to them giving details of how to find your home in the village of Steeply Hill.

Activities

1 Study the map shown in **Appendix 1**. Your friend will be driving and entering the village on the **B1818** at the north end of the village.

2 Plan the route to be taken to your home which is **No 17 Greys Mews**. Remember to mention road names and any landmarks which will be of extra help to your friend.

3 Write a personal letter to your friend – **remember your address is 17 Greys Mews, Steeply Hill** (you can make up a County and a post code) giving him/her directions once they enter the village from the north.

   Include some general comment(s) about being pleased he/she is coming to stay and naming the day and date of arrival, which is next Friday.

4 You can finish the letter with an informal close like "Best Wishes", or "Kind Regards".

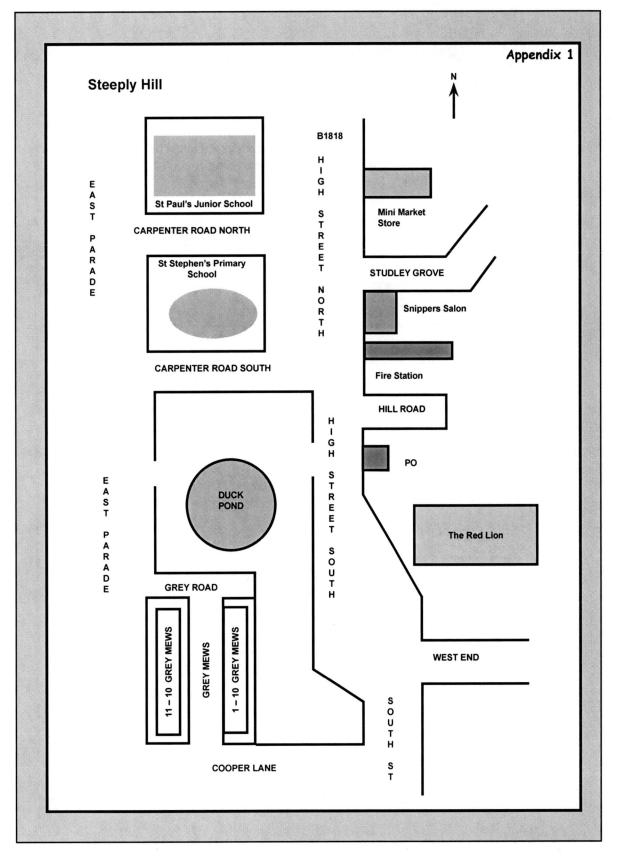

Appendix 1

Steeply Hill

Task 16: Another Brick in the Wall — Property Sales

<table>
<tr>
<td>

Student Information

In this task you will interpret information illustrated in a bar chart and write a memo.

Ask your tutor for a copy of the **Another Brick in the Wall** memo sheet.

</td>
<td>

REMEMBER

Look at the **keys** to the information and the **legend** on the chart to help you understand the information the chart displays.

See "Reading and Understanding Information Displayed in Charts" on page 89.

Your memo should be brief and you must sign it.

See "Writing and Setting Out Memos" on page 80.

</td>
</tr>
</table>

Interpreting a Chart and Writing a Memo

Scenario

Jasper Bennett of the building company **Another Brick in the Wall** needs some information for a meeting he is attending next week. You have to supply him with this information.

Activities

In **Task 10** you dealt with a telephone message for Jasper Bennett which indicated he is attending a site meeting next week. In this task you have to supply him with some sales figures before his meeting.

1   Study the bar chart shown in **Appendix 1**.

2   Jasper wants you to tell him, **for each of the four sites the company is working on in the village of Ashcombe** :

-      how many properties have been built; and

-      how many of those properties have been sold.

Put this information in a memo to him. Jasper is the Development Manager of the company.

Use a heading for the Memo: Ashcombe Village Developments

Date the Memo today, send it from yourself and sign it.

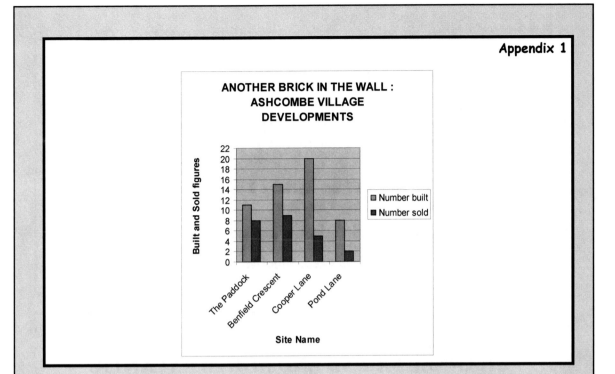

Appendix 1

ANOTHER BRICK IN THE WALL :
ASHCOMBE VILLAGE
DEVELOPMENTS

Task 17: Polkerith Post Newspaper — Completing an Article

Student Information	REMEMBER
In this task you will study information given to you and use some of it to complete a newspaper article. Ask your tutor for the newspaper Article — shown in **Appendix 1**.	Read the instructions carefully so you understand what you have to do. Read the text carefully so you know what information you have to include from the tables. Study the tables carefully so you understand which information you have to select. See *"Reading and Understanding Information Displayed in Tables"* on page 87.

Interpreting Information from Tables and Completing a Newspaper Article

Scenario

You work in the Sports Department of the Polkerith Post which is a local daily newspaper based in Padstow, Cornwall. The Sports Editor is Peter Mariner and he has begun an article and asked you to complete it for him, adding details of race winners and times.

Activities

1   Read the article shown in **Appendix 1** so that you know the information you need to add.

2   Study **Tables A and B** – shown in **Appendix 2** – and make a note, for both races, of the yachts which came **1st**, **2nd** and **last** and their race times.

3   Include the information from **Activity 2** in the appropriate parts of the article written by Peter Mariner.

Note: the race times represent minutes and seconds.

Hand in the article you have completed, **together with** the notes you made in **Activity 2**.

Appendix 1

CHANNEL ISLAND AND NORTH ATLANTIC YACHT RACE

The first day of the Channel Island and North Atlantic Yacht Race saw some spectacular racing, particularly between the Channel Islanders and their French team competitors.

Despite rough conditions for the morning race, starting at   which took place **West of Alderney**, the yachts finishing in first and third place were separated by only 27 seconds.

In **first place** was the Channel Island yacht   captained by Jack Windsome (47) and his crew Saul Windsor (27) and Henry Kingdom (33). Although this was in an excellent time of   minutes and   seconds, it was not the fastest in the 29-year history of the race – this title is still held by the Jersey-based yacht Estrella da Mar which, in 1996, completed the course, under similar blustery conditions, in 10 minutes and 31 seconds.

The longer-distance race – **East of Sark** – began at 1400 hours and was won by   in a time of   . Twelve yachts took part and the yacht placed **last** was   which completed the course in 14 minutes and 18 seconds. In **second place** was   with a winning time of

It was a good day's racing and I'll be reporting the highlights of the races today and tomorrow plus summarising an interview with Jack Windsome.

Peter Mariner

CHANNEL ISLAND AND NORTH ATLANTIC YACHT RACE

COURSE "A" – WEST OF ALDERNEY

RACE RESULTS   DAY 1

(Yesterday's date)   1030 hours

Channel Island Competitors		French Competitors	
Yacht	Race Time	Yacht	Race Time
Swing	10:46	South Wind	10:53
Lola IV	11:13	Misty Me	11:21
Gato Preto	11:34	Baixo	11:37
Avanti	11:39	Radio Waves	11:50
Supressa	11:56	Lady Lavender	12:23
Devonia	13:14	Madam Cass	12:57

COURSE "B" – EAST OF SARK

RACE RESULTS   DAY 1

(Yesterday's date)   1400 hours

Channel Island Competitors		English Competitors	
Yacht	Race Time	Yacht	Race Time
Swing	12:26	Quarter Moon	12:18
Avanti	12:38	Who Knows?	12:36
Peggy Sue	12:59	Cavalier	12:48
Guernsey Cream	13:08	Sorondongo	12:49
Tiempo	13:24	Passion Fruit	13:04
Storm Cloud	13:40	Whiskers	14:18

Task 18: Sunny Destinations Travel — Selecting Holiday Accommodation

Student Information	REMEMBER
In this task you will study information given to you and write a fax. Ask your tutor for a blank **Sunny Destinations** fax sheet.	A fax is an official document, but it can be seen by anyone who comes across it on the fax machine. Be careful, therefore, not to be any less formal than in other business documents — just treat it like a letter that is delivered more quickly! See "Reading and Understanding Information Displayed in Tables" on page 87. See "Sending Faxes" on page 106. Make sure the information you include is accurate and appropriate and your handwriting is neat.

Interpreting Information and Writing a Fax

Scenario

You work for Sunny Destinations Travel and have received, overnight, a telephone message left on the company's answering machine from a potential customer. You are to answer the questions and write a fax to send to the caller.

Activities

1 Read the note of the telephone message – shown in **Appendix 1**

2 Using the information from the database – shown in **Appendix 2** – highlight the accommodation which meets the client's requirements.

3 Compose a fax to be sent to the client which contains details of the accommodation you recommend as appropriate. Include **any other information** you think he will need to know - flight times, etc.

4 You can write and sign the fax with your name.

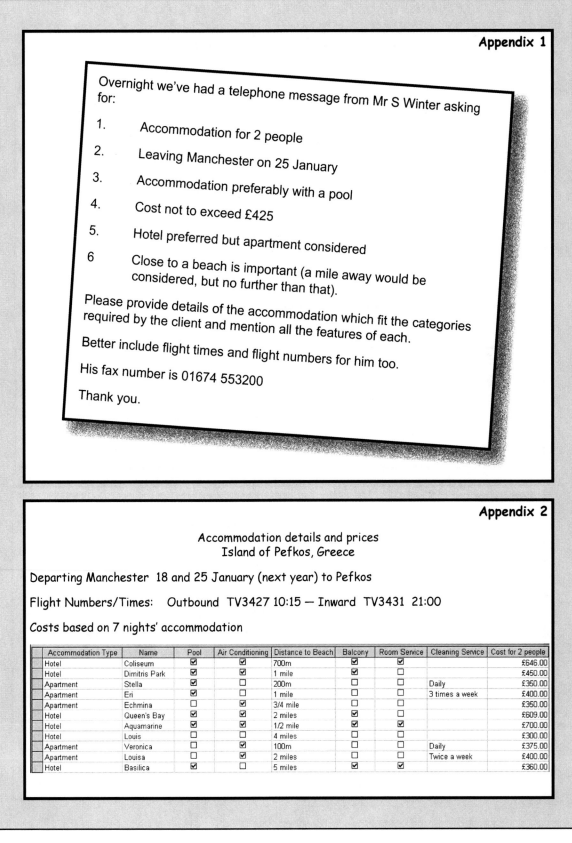

Appendix 1

Overnight we've had a telephone message from Mr S Winter asking for:

1. Accommodation for 2 people

2. Leaving Manchester on 25 January

3. Accommodation preferably with a pool

4. Cost not to exceed £425

5. Hotel preferred but apartment considered

6. Close to a beach is important (a mile away would be considered, but no further than that).

Please provide details of the accommodation which fit the categories required by the client and mention all the features of each.

Better include flight times and flight numbers for him too.

His fax number is 01674 553200

Thank you.

Appendix 2

Accommodation details and prices
Island of Pefkos, Greece

Departing Manchester 18 and 25 January (next year) to Pefkos

Flight Numbers/Times: Outbound TV3427 10:15 — Inward TV3431 21:00

Costs based on 7 nights' accommodation

Accommodation Type	Name	Pool	Air Conditioning	Distance to Beach	Balcony	Room Service	Cleaning Service	Cost for 2 people
Hotel	Coliseum	☑	☑	700m	☑	☑		£646.00
Hotel	Dimitris Park	☑	☑	1 mile	☑	☐		£450.00
Apartment	Stella	☑	☐	200m	☐	☐	Daily	£350.00
Apartment	Eri	☑	☐	1 mile	☐	☐	3 times a week	£400.00
Apartment	Echmina	☐	☑	3/4 mile	☐	☐		£350.00
Hotel	Queen's Bay	☑	☑	2 miles	☑	☐		£609.00
Hotel	Aquamarine	☑	☑	1/2 mile	☑	☑		£700.00
Hotel	Louis	☐	☐	4 miles	☐	☐		£300.00
Apartment	Veronica	☐	☑	100m	☐	☐	Daily	£375.00
Apartment	Louisa	☐	☑	2 miles	☐	☐	Twice a week	£400.00
Hotel	Basilica	☑	☐	5 miles	☑	☑		£360.00

Task 19: Polkerith Post Newspaper — Researching a Holiday Destination

Student Information	REMEMBER
In this task you will research information.	Include your research documents with the task you hand to your tutor.
You will also write a memo.	*If you cannot do this, take a photocopy of the documents you find, and attach a copy to this task.*
Ask your tutor for a **Polkerith Post** memo sheet.	*See "Writing and Setting Out Memos" on page 80.*
	If you include images, they must help the reader understand the topic.
	See "Using Images in Communication" on page 91.

Conducting Research and Writing a Memo

Scenario

Next year is the 30th Anniversary of the "Channel Island and North Atlantic Yacht Race". A 30th anniversary is a **pearl** anniversary so the yacht race is going to be based around the island known as the Pearl of the Atlantic, Madeira. You are now to do some research so that Peter Mariner can write an article for the Polkerith Post.

Activities

1   Carry out some research into the island of Madeira so you have information on each of the following :

-    where the island is situated

-    the size of the island

-    with which country the island is associated

-    usual temperatures in the month of July (the month when the race will take place).

If you plan to use the Internet as one of your methods of research you might visit the following websites:

   www.madeira-web.com/madeira.html

   www.madeira-tourist.com/page33/page33.html

   www.holiday-weather.com/madeira/averages

2   Write a memo to Peter Mariner the Sports Editor, setting out your findings.

     Use the heading **SOME FACTS ON THE ISLAND OF MADEIRA** and include an introductory paragraph which says you have found the information he asked for and this is shown below.

3   Add a final paragraph which offers further help if he needs more information.

4   Sign the memo and hand it, and your research documents, to your tutor.

Task 20: Polkerith Post Newspaper — The Race Results

Student Information	REMEMBER
In this task you will study information given to you and transfer some information into a table.	Read the instructions and the tables carefully so you understand what you have to do.
	See "Reading and Understanding Information Displayed in Tables" on page 87.
Ask your tutor for 3 blank **Race Results** sheets.	Make sure the information you write is accurate and that your handwriting is legible.

Interpreting and Extracting Information and Completing a Table

Scenario

The Polkerith Post will print the results of the Channel Island and North Atlantic Yacht Race and you have to prepare this information.

Activities

In **Task 17** you had information about the results of the first day's racing in the Channel Islands and North Atlantic Yacht Race. Now Peter Mariner has given you information on all six races over days 1, 2 and 3 – **shown in Appendix 1** - and asked you to add the relevant details to a table so these can be published in tomorrow's paper.

1   Ask your tutor for three copies of the **Race Results** sheet, an example of which is shown in **Appendix 2**.

2 Complete the Race Summary sheets with the required information extracted from the tables.

Note: the 1st place result of the first race on the first day has been completed in the example as a guide for you.

Appendix 1

CHANNEL ISLAND AND NORTH ATLANTIC YACHT RACE

COURSE "A" — WEST OF ALDERNEY
RACE RESULTS DAY 1
(date) 1030 hours

Channel Island Competitors		French Competitors	
Yacht	Race Time	Yacht	Race Time
Swing	10:46	South Wind	10:53
Lola IV	11:13	Misty Me	11:21
Gato Preto	11:34	Baixo	11:37
Avanti	11:39	Radio Waves	11:50
Supressa	11:56	Lady Lavender	12:23
Devonia	13:14	Madam Cass	12:57

COURSE "B" - EAST OF SARK
RACE RESULTS DAY 1
(date) 1400 hours

Channel Island Competitors		English Competitors	
Yacht	Race Time	Yacht	Race Time
Swing	12:26	Quarter Moon	12:18
Avanti	12:38	Who Knows?	12:36
Peggy Sue	12:59	Mr Seth	12:48
Guernsey Cream	13:08	Sorondongo	12:49
Tiempo	13:24	Passion Fruit	13:04
Storm Cloud	13:40	Whiskers	14:18

RACE RESULTS DAY 2
(date) 1100 hours

English Competitors		French Competitors	
Yacht	Race Time	Yacht	Race Time
Quarter Moon	11:01	River Seine	11:26
Who Knows?	11:21	Fleetline	11:29
Prince Charming	11:41	Lady Lavender	11:55
Genuine Article	12:06	Baixo	12:16
Gato Preto	12:09	Red Wine	12:34
Bluebell	12:50	Madam Cass	13:08

RACE RESULTS DAY 2
(date) 1430hours

Channel Island Competitors		French Competitors	
Yacht	Race Time	Yacht	Race Time
Devonia	12:35	South Wind	12:20
Avanti	12:38	Red Wine	12:29
Mr Marmalade	13:08	High Regard	12:48
Guernsey Cream	13:15	Neptune IV	12:54
Ladybird	13:25	Misty Me	13:46
Black Cat	13:56	Bobbykins	13:52

CHANNEL ISLAND AND NORTH ATLANTIC YACHT RACE

COURSE "A" — WEST OF ALDERNEY
RACE RESULTS   DAY 3
(date)   1030 hours

English Competitors		Channel Island Competitors	
Yacht	Race Time	Yacht	Race Time
Who Knows?	10:35	Island Dream	10:32
Prince Charming	11:18	Mr Marmalade	11:02
Quarter Moon	11:49	Guernsey Cream	11:45
Dick Turpin	12:18	Solomon II	12:39
Summer Breeze	12:27	Greystone Rock	13:11
Passion Fruit	13:08	Jack and Jill	13:28

COURSE "B" — EAST OF SARK
RACE RESULTS   DAY 3
(date)   1500 hours

Channel Island Competitors		French Competitors	
Yacht	Race Time	Yacht	Race Time
Lola IV	12:08	South Wind	12:20
Cruising Lady	12:27	Red Wine	12:29
Venture Maid	12:55	The Empress Claudia	12:50
Guernsey Cream	13:15	Bobbykins	13:09
Island Hopper	13:17	California Dreamin'	13:38
A to Z	14:07	March Wind	13:57

Appendix 2

RACE RESULTS SHEET

Day 1	insert the appropriate day and date (3 days ago, then 2 days ago then yesterday)
Start Time	
Course	insert whether Course A or Course B

Place	Race Time	Yacht	Nationality
1st	10:46	Swing	Channel Islander
2nd			
3rd			
6th			

Day 1	insert the appropriate day and date (3 days ago, then 2 days ago then yesterday)
Start Time	
Course	insert whether Course A or Course B

Place	Race Time	Yacht	Nationality
1st			
2nd			
3rd			
6th			

Task 21: Sunny Destinations Travel — Arranging an Advertisement

Student Information	REMEMBER
In this task you will display an advertisement and write a memo.	Be consistent with how you express similar information.
Ask your tutor for a blank **Sunny Destinations** memo sheet and a **Sunny Destinations** logo sheet.	Your memo should be brief and you must sign it.
	See "Writing Advertisements" on page 94.
	See "Writing and Setting Out Memos" on page 80.

Interpreting Information, Writing an Advertisement and Writing a Memo

Scenario

As next year is a special year in the history of the "Channel Island and North Atlantic Yacht Race", Sunny Destinations Travel has been asked by the Channel Island Yacht Club to organise travel and accommodation to the island of Madeira. You have to display an advertisement which will eventually appear in the local newspaper — Polkerith Post.

Activities

The Advertising Editor of Sunny Destinations Travel (Mrs Daisy Flowers) has drafted the wording of the advertisement - **Appendix 1**.

1   Organise the information so it is in a logical order. Don't worry too much about the display because once it goes to the newspaper, they will display it for you. You can use the Sunny Destinations logo sheet if you wish.

2   Write a Memo to Daisy Flowers (don't forget to include her title), saying you have drafted the advertisement and are attaching it to this memo. Say you are happy to make any alterations she may require.

Attach your advertisement to the Memo you write.

Appendix 1

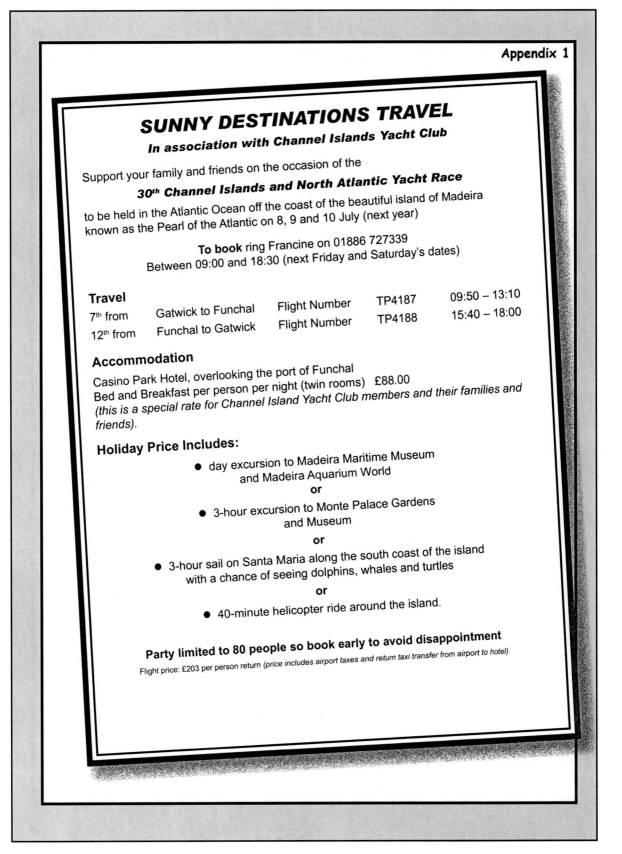

SUNNY DESTINATIONS TRAVEL
In association with Channel Islands Yacht Club

Support your family and friends on the occasion of the

30th Channel Islands and North Atlantic Yacht Race

to be held in the Atlantic Ocean off the coast of the beautiful island of Madeira known as the Pearl of the Atlantic on 8, 9 and 10 July (next year)

To book ring Francine on 01886 727339
Between 09:00 and 18:30 (next Friday and Saturday's dates)

Travel

7th from	Gatwick to Funchal	Flight Number	TP4187	09:50 – 13:10
12th from	Funchal to Gatwick	Flight Number	TP4188	15:40 – 18:00

Accommodation

Casino Park Hotel, overlooking the port of Funchal
Bed and Breakfast per person per night (twin rooms) £88.00
(this is a special rate for Channel Island Yacht Club members and their families and friends).

Holiday Price Includes:

- day excursion to Madeira Maritime Museum
  and Madeira Aquarium World

  or

- 3-hour excursion to Monte Palace Gardens
  and Museum

  or

- 3-hour sail on Santa Maria along the south coast of the island
  with a chance of seeing dolphins, whales and turtles

  or

- 40-minute helicopter ride around the island.

Party limited to 80 people so book early to avoid disappointment

Flight price: £203 per person return (price includes airport taxes and return taxi transfer from airport to hotel)

Task 22: Sunny Destinations Travel — Placing an Advertisement

Student Information	REMEMBER
In this task you will write to a newspaper to ask them to place an advertisement for you. Ask your tutor for a blank **Sunny Destinations** letter heading.	A business letter is a formal document. *See "Writing and Setting Out Business Letters" on page 97 and "Useful Phrases for Business Letters" on page 100.* Make sure your letter contains the following: - the date it was written; - the title, name and address of the person who will receive the letter; - a salutation (Dear ?); - a complimentary close that matches the salutation; - the name of the person who wrote the letter. Be sure to sign the letter.

Writing a Business Letter

Scenario

In **Task 21** you wrote an advertisement for Daisy Flowers to consider. Now you have to arrange for that advertisement to appear in the local newspaper.

Activities

Daisy is happy with the advertisement you produced in **Task 21** and now she wants you to arrange for it to appear in the local newspaper — Polkerith Post.

1   Write to the Advertising Manager of the Polkerith Post, arranging the following:

a)   the advertisement to appear on Tuesday and Wednesday of next week (be specific about the dates);

b)   ask for it to appear as a quarter-page advertisement;

c)   the account is to be sent to the Accounts Manager of the travel agency who is Sajeel Ahmed.

Note: the name of the Advertising Manager is Lewis Aubin and Polkerith Post's address is Martindale House, Ocean View, Padstow, Cornwall PD2 2KD.

Task 23: Palm Trees Hotel — Organising Conference Members

Student Information	REMEMBER
In this task you will read instructions and interpret information. You will use this information to create a new table of information.	Make sure your writing is clear and neat and all names are spelt correctly and can be read easily. See *"Reading and Understanding Information Displayed in Tables"* on page 87. See *"Arranging Text in Alphabetical Order"* on page 72.

Interpreting Information and Creating Tabular Information

Scenario

A conference is being held over three days in the Palm Trees Hotel where you work. You have to help with organising the event.

Activities

The Conference Manager — Rebecca Monmouth — has given you the list of the 30 people **(Appendix 1)** who are attending the conference your hotel is hosting for the international company ALTO NETWORK. She has asked you to deal with a number of tasks on her behalf.

1   Alto Network has asked for conference rooms and Rebecca has allocated the following:

     1   Dublin Suite

     2   Caracas Suite

     3   Edinburgh Suite

     4   Prague Suite

     5   Athens Suite.

     As you are going to arrange the names of the delegates into the Suites, prepare a table with headings, similar to the one shown in **Appendix 2. At this stage DO NOT** enter the delegates' names just the suite names.

2   Alto Network has sent a fax today and Rebecca has written a note on it for you. **The fax is Appendix 3.** Read it so you understand the content and know what Rebecca has asked you to do.

3   Arrange the names as requested, placing them in the Suites starting with Suite 1 and continuing to Suite 5.

Make sure you put the **surname first**.

Hand in the lists from Activities 2 and 3 to your tutor.

Appendix 1

1	2	3	4	5
Milly Tavistock	Ben Barnes	Bradley Garbutt	Alan Sharpe	Ethan Squires
Jon Hawks	Lewis Cherrett	Eamonn Price	Martin Stobbart	Dale Butterfield
Stewart Marley	Jen Luckhurst	Mae Phipps	Erin Milton	Daisy Clement
Ivor Plann	Aimee Johnston	Reece Parsons	Jonathan Fellows	Dougall Grey
Pamela Baines	Pula Swartz	Iva Glass	Kyle Feathers	Beth Greystone
Leanne Carpenter	Zak Chesterton	Keelie Reid	Shariq Mussatt	Ethan Knowles

Appendix 2

Name of Suite	Delegates' Names
1 Dublin Suite	*delegates' names go here*
2 Caracas Suite	*delegates' names go here*

Fax

ALTO NETWORK

For:	Rebecca Monmouth, Palm Trees Hotel
Fax number:	01328 882900
From:	Ivan Petrovich, Conference Manager, Alto Network
Fax number:	01552 343291
Date:	(Today's date)
Regarding:	Conference at your hotel 8th — 10th (next month) 2010
No. of pages: 1	

Comments:

I sent you a list of delegates split into Groups 1-5 a few days ago. I have changed my mind and now would like the names put into alphabetical surname order.

Please could you organise this into a table which can be given to each delegate?

Ivan

I've checked with Ivan and am clear about what he wants now.

Could you arrange all names on the list so they are in alphabetical order of surname (A–Z), then in the table, put the first 6 into the first suite, the second 6 into the second suite etc. etc.

Thank you

Rebecca

Task 24: Palm Trees Hotel — Confirming Conference Arrangements

Student Information	REMEMBER
In this task you will write a memo and attach work you did in **Task 23**. Ask your Tutor for a **Palm Trees Hotel** memo sheet.	Your memo should be brief and contain relevant and accurate information. *See "Writing and Setting Out Memos" on page 80.*

Writing a Memo

Scenario

In **Task 23** you arranged the delegates' names as instructed by Mrs Rebecca Monmouth. Now you have to send her a memo to which you will attach these details.

Activities

1 Write a memo to Rebecca Monmouth, Conference Manager, using the heading **ALTO NETWORK CONFERENCE 8TH — 10TH** *(next month) - DELEGATE GROUPS*

Say you have done as she asked and now attach the document which shows the delegates arranged into groups and conference rooms.

Attach the work you prepared in **Task 23** to the memo and hand to your tutor.

Don't forget to sign the memo.

Jason

Task 25: 1925 Restaurant — Planning a Menu

Student Information	REMEMBER
In this task you will conduct some research and write a memo.	Keep your memo brief and don't forget to sign it.
	See "Writing and Setting Out Memos" on page 80.
Ask your tutor for a blank **1925 Restaurant** memo sheet.	You need to attach your recommended recipes to the task you hand to your tutor.
	Include the printouts or take a photocopy of the documents you find.

Conducting Research and Writing a Memo

Scenario

You work for 1925 Restaurant and the Head Chef, Alberto Safira, is thinking about arranging a "European Celebration Dinner" next month. You have been asked to find recipes relating to three European countries and send them to him with a covering memo.

Activities

1   Read the memo from Alberto Safira — shown in **Appendix 1**.

2   Using appropriate web sites and reference sources, find and print out/ photocopy the required details.

3   Write a memo, in reply to the one from Alberto, saying you are attaching the recipes you have found which you think are appropriate.

      Begin by thanking him for his memo.

      You might want to give the title of the recipes and the country associated with each. It's up to you.

4   Attach to the memo the recipes you think are suitable.

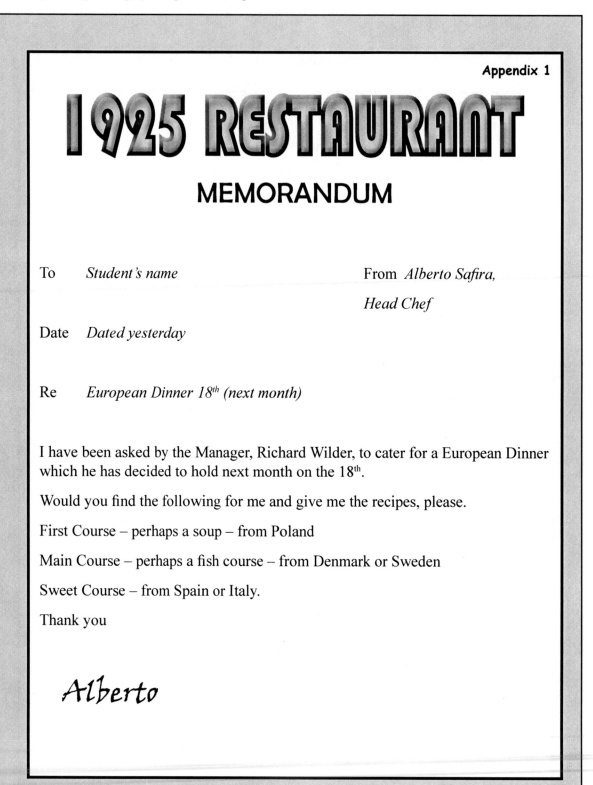

Task 26: Vroom Vroom Motor Traders — Vehicle Recall

Student Information	REMEMBER
In this task you will study instructions and information from a database and compose an email to a colleague. Ask your tutor for the blank **Vroom Vroom** email document.	Read the documents and the instructions carefully so you are clear about what you have to do. See *"Reading and Understanding Information Displayed in Tables"* on page 87. Make sure what you write is accurate. An email to a colleague may use informal language but correct spelling, grammar and punctuation are still important.

Interpreting Information and Writing an Email

Scenario

Vroom Vroom Motor Traders is a main Citroën dealer in the Solihull area of England. Citroën has written to the company notifying them of a vehicle recall.

Activities

Citroën has become aware of a problem with some C2 models, first registered between March and June 2007. Vehicles meeting this description need to be recalled for repair.

1   Read the Press Notice which Vroom Vroom published yesterday in the local newspaper — **Appendix 1**.

2   The Warranty Repair Manager, Vic Vaux, has written a note to you which contains some instructions — **Appendix 2**.

Read the note and from the database, **Appendix 3**, make a note of those cars which will have to be recalled and the customer to whom they belong.

3   Once you have the information required by Vic, put your findings in an email to him. Your tutor will give you the email document to which you can add your message.

Appendix 1

VROOM VROOM MOTOR TRADER

Lizardpark Farm Trading Estate

SOLIHULL SL4 9BA

YOUR LOCAL CITROËN MAIN DEALER

RECALL   RECALL   RECALL   RECALL   RECALL

ANNOUNCEMENT

CITROËN HAS RECENTLY ANNOUNCED AN ESSENTIAL RECALL ON SELECTED VEHICLES OF THE MODEL C2

THIS AFFECTS SOME VEHICLES FIRST REGISTERED BETWEEN MARCH AND JUNE 2007

THE FAULT IS RELATED TO THE TRACK ROD END

IT IS IMPORTANT TO REALISE

NOT ALL VEHICLES WILL BE AFFECTED

BUT

ALL VEHICLES MUST BE CHECKED

IF YOUR V.I.N. NUMBER BEGINS WITH THE DIGITS 4078

AND YOUR VEHICLE WAS FIRST REGISTERED

BETWEEN 1st MARCH AND 30th JUNE 2007

THEN CONTACT US IMMEDIATELY AND BOOK YOUR VEHICLE IN FOR INSPECTION

INSPECTION AND REPLACEMENT, IF NECESSARY, WILL TAKE ONE HOUR

CONTACT US ON 01877 4359018

DO IT TODAY

Today's date

After the Recall Notice from Citroen and the advertisement we put in the local newspaper yesterday, I need to know which customers and cars are involved in this recall.

Would you check the database attached and email me with details of the Customer Reference, Car Registration Number and Registration Date.

Thank you
Vic

Customer Details : Citroen C2 : Table

Customer Reference	Vin No	Reg Date	Reg No
103	455961381	01 March 2007	SB07 TTW
104	407833702	02 March 2007	SB07 JKH
105	407735240	03 March 2007	SB07 JKJ
106	405276511	16 March 2007	SB07 WWK
111	409265422	17 March 2007	SB07 LLY
108	407832989	21 March 2007	SB07 LLW
109	407827611	23 March 2007	SB07 STH
124	409269978	23 March 2007	SB07 RMK
121	407832382	05 April 2007	SB07 JJN
122	407739144	15 April 2007	SB07 WXW
139	405267627	23 April 2007	SB07 YNY
130	407827762	30 April 2007	SB07 YXC
125	407335926	05 May 2007	SB07 JJP
109	407838321	16 May 2007	SB07 WNB
137	407823550	26 May 2007	SB07 GRB
146	407835528	03 June 2007	SB07 BVS
156	407282454	15 June 1007	SB07 RNH

Task 27: Plane Designs — A Sales Advertisement

Student Information	REMEMBER
In this task you will write an advertising flyer. Ask your tutor for a **Plane Designs** logo sheet.	Correct spelling, grammar and punctuation are important. If you use an image with the text make sure the image is appropriate and helps the reader to understand the document. "Using Images in Communication" on page 91. See "Writing Advertisements" on page 94.

Writing an Advertising Flyer

Scenario

Plane Designs, a joinery firm, regularly offers special deals in order to attract customers. This task involves advertising such a deal.

Activities

You work for Plane Designs joinery firm, and its owner, Peter Dawson, wants to advertise a special deal related to wooden doors for houses. He has given you some information and wants you to prepare the advertisement which will eventually be printed on A4 paper by a local printing company and then distributed to households in the local area.

1   Read Peter's note in **Appendix 1**.

2   Plan the wording and layout of the advertising flyer. If you use a computer to do this you might want to include an image to enhance the readers' understanding of what is being advertised.

The finished flyer must go onto the **Plane Designs** logo sheet which your tutor will give you.

Appendix 1

Wooden Door Clearance Sale

Buy one wooden front door and we'll provide a back door free*.

Solid, hardwood doors, with mortice locks cost as little as £175 up to £300 (excluding door furniture).

<u>Range</u>

The Ewbank	£175	The Marquis	£189
The Hallington	£195	The Embassy	£220
The Imperial	£245	The Cavendish	£270
The Hartley	£300		

<u>Door Furniture</u>   Handles, letterboxes and numbers available in brass, silver chrome or white plastic. Prices start from £20.99 for white plastic to £49.99 for brass.

Call for a brochure or visit the showroom - open between 9am and 4pm Monday to Thursday.

* Back door supplied is The Hallington

We've rather a lot of wooden doors for houses in stock and I want rid of them. It's time to offer them as a special deal to customers.

I've written the details of the offer which will be professionally printed on A4 paper and then distributed to households in the area. Can you tidy it up please and arrange is a sensible order for me? Don't worry too much about the display as the printing firm will do this better than we can.

Thank you

Peter

Task 28: Vroom Vroom Motor Traders — Booking a Car in for Inspection

Student Information	REMEMBER
In this task you will take the part of a garage's Workshop Receptionist and book in a customer's car for inspection. Ask your tutor for a copy of the **Booking Sheets** before you begin this task.	*See "Using the Telephone and Making Telephone Calls" on page 104.* You will need to introduce yourself and your company when you answer the telephone call. End the call politely.

Taking Part in a Telephone Call with a Customer

Scenario

As a result of the recall advertisement placed in the local paper by Vroom Vroom, a customer rings today to book his/her car in for an inspection.

Activities

The notice about Citroën recall, which was the basis of **Task 26**, has had an effect, and today a customer rings you to book his/her car in for inspection.

Your tutor will take the part of the customer who telephones to say they have seen the notice in the newspaper and their car needs to be inspected.

NOTE: You will need a copy of the email you sent to Vic Vaux in Task 26.

When you take the call, you will need to refer to the "Booking Sheets". (An <u>extract</u> is shown in Appendix 1.)

1   Enter the appropriate dates on both Booking Sheets.

2   When your tutor rings, and you have introduced yourself at the start of the call, the information you will need from the caller is:

  -    the car registration number (so you can locate the vehicle on the list contained in the email to Vic Vaux);

- the customer's name and contact details;

- when the customer wishes the car to be inspected (refer to the **Booking Sheets** when dealing with this as you can only accept, or offer, times that are available).

You can possibly expect the caller to be anxious but will need to reassure him/her the vehicle is safe and may not even need to be repaired. The appointment will be for one hour.

3   When the arrangements have been made, confirm the day and time clearly to the customer so there is no doubt about the booking.

4   Once the appointment has been made, enter the necessary details on the Booking Sheet.

Hand the booking sheets to your tutor.

Appendix 1

VROOM VROOM VEHICLE REPAIR/SERVICE

BOOKING SHEET

CITROËN RECALL INSPECTION/REPAIR SHEET

Day and Date	Time	Vehicle Registration Number	Customer's Name and Contact Details
Monday (*next Monday's date*)			
	0830 – 0930	SB07 BVS	Mr Todmorton 01877 334921
	0945 – 1045		
	1100 – 1200	SB07 YXC	Dr Sample 01757 354888
	1330 – 1430		
	1445 – 1545		
	1600 – 1700		
Tuesday (*next Tuesday's date*)			

Task 29: Larchfield Village Council — No Cold Callers Thank You

Student Information	REMEMBER
In this task you will take the part of an employee of Larchfield Village Council and take a telephone request from a resident.	You will need to introduce yourself and mention your Council's name when you answer the telephone call.
Ask your tutor for a copy of the **Distribution Sheet** before you begin this task.	End the call politely.
	See "Using the Telephone and Making Telephone Calls" on page 104.

Taking Part in a Telephone Call

Scenario

The Village Council has posted advertising flyers in householders' letterboxes in the village and, as a result, telephone requests for window stickers are now being received.

Activities

Larchfield Village Council has recently introduced a scheme which is described in the information leaflet shown in **Appendix 1**.

Today you take a telephone call requesting a window sticker.

1.   Get the **Distribution Sheet** from your tutor before you begin this task. You will need to complete this with the caller's details so the Council has a record of which householder has requested a window sticker. Enter the correct dates in the first column.

2.   Your tutor will take the part of the caller who will request a window sticker. You need, from the caller, the information shown on the Distribution Sheet.

   Be polite and remember to repeat the caller's details so you check you have the information correctly.

3.   Say the sticker will be delivered to the caller's home within the next two days.

Hand the completed Distribution Sheet to your tutor.

LEAFLET NUMBER 103

LARCHFIELD VILLAGE COUNCIL

BOGUS CALLERS AND DISTRACTION BURGLARIES

This type of crime is where someone "cold calls" pretending to be from an organisation such as the Water Board, the Electricity Board or some other housing-related organisation. The caller aims to gain entry to your property and then usually a second person enters and theft occurs as the first person distracts the home owner. Victims are generally the elderly and this section of our community is more likely to believe the criminal who may be wearing a suit and equipped with clipboards, forms and even false identification.

There has been an increase in this type of crime in Larchfield so to help prevent this Larchfield Village Council is offering a

Free Window Sticker Stating

NO COLD CALLERS THANK YOU

To get your free Window Sticker Telephone Marcia on 01677 326600

Place your Window Sticker on the inside of the glass of your front door, or in a window near the front door. **If you have any doubts about a caller tell your Neighbourhood Watch Co-ordinator Paul Williams who can be contacted on 01773 562077.**

Task 30: Gigs Galore — Arranging a Band's UK Tour Itinerary

Student Information	REMEMBER
In this task you will work with a partner to plan a UK itinerary for a band's tour. Ask your tutor for a copy of the **Partnership Discussion Form** before you begin this task.	When working with a partner make sure you contribute to the discussions and the decision-making process. Encourage your partner to contribute. Speak politely and express your views clearly. See "Taking Part in a Formal, or an Informal Discussion" on page 126.

Working with a Partner and Planning an Itinerary

Scenario

You work in the office of **Gigs Galore**, a company which organises and promotes national tours of bands. Today you are involved in planning the tour of a new, but popular, local band.

Activities

1   **With a partner**, think of a name for a band. This will have to be something you can illustrate in **Task 31**. Therefore think before choosing something like "Black Nights" as it's uncertain how you could illustrate this!!

2   **Individually** make notes on the first part of your Partnership Discussion Form which summarises your work and discussion so far.

3   **Working with your partner**, refer to the venue details shown in **Appendix 1**, and plan the route for the 11-day UK tour, beginning in the town/city nearest to where you are in the country, and travelling the least distance from **venue to venue**.

> NOTE: the band performs on alternate days, travelling and resting on the following day.
>
> The tour *begins* at a venue on the 3rd of next month.

4	Display the venue details using the headings :

Band's Name

UK Tour: 3rd to 23rd (next month)

Date   Venue   Town/City

5	**Individually** complete the rest of your Partnership Discussion form and hand this in with Task 4's work.

Appendix 1

Town/City	Venue
Birmingham	City Hall
Brighton	Forum Theatre
Chelmsford	Wharton Park
Glasgow	City Hall
Lincoln	City Gardens
Newcastle	The Sage Centre
Oxford	Culpepper Building
Reading	Riverside Hall
Sheffield	The Sheffield Arena
Taunton	The Guildhall
York	The Barbican

Task 31: Gigs Galore — Advertising the UK Tour

Student Information	REMEMBER
In this task you will prepare an illustrated Advertising Flyer.	Correct spelling, grammar and punctuation are important. When you use an image with text make sure the image is appropriate. See "Using Images in Communication" on page 91. See "Writing Advertisements" on page 94.

Designing an Advertisement

Scenario

Your work in **Task 30** now leads you to preparing an advertisement for the Band's UK tour next month.

Activities

1 Using the Itinerary you produced in **Task 30**, and thinking about the band's name and how to illustrate it, design an advertisement which will appear in the specialist music magazines later this month.

You must mention every venue being played as well as the dates.

Other information to decide upon and include is :

   – the price of the tickets (this will be the same for each venue);

   – the time of the performance (this will be the same for each venue);

   – how, and where, to buy the tickets and when they will be on sale.

Add any other information you feel necessary but be careful not to clutter the advertisement with unnecessary information as this will prevent it from being understood and possibly even read!

Task 32: Jack and Jill's Children's Nursery — A Child is Unwell

Student Information	REMEMBER
In this task you will telephone a parent to request they collect their sick child.	See "Using the Telephone and Making Telephone Calls" on page 104. You will need to introduce yourself and the Nursery when the telephone is answered. End the call politely.

Making a Telephone Call

Scenario

You work in Jack and Jill Children's Nursery and have to telephone a parent today to report their child is unwell and request that the child be collected from the nursery.

Activities

Your tutor will take the part of the person answering the telephone call.

Decide on a child's name (male or female) and assume the person you are calling is the mother/father with the same surname as the child.

1   Plan what you will say – it will be important not to alarm the parent. You will aim to :

-    state the child's name (their son or daughter);

-    say the child (use the name) has been vomiting (three times in the last two hours);

-    say there is no rash but the child seems to have a high temperature;

-    request the child be collected from the Nursery as soon as possible, preferably within the next hour.

2   If asked by the parent you have not called a doctor but you have isolated the child and a member of staff is sitting with him/her.

Task 33: Isaac Newton Airport — Enquiring About Flights

Student Information	REMEMBER
In this task you will interpret information in tables then take a telephone call asking about flights to Paris.	Read the timetables so you will be able to find the information for which you will be asked.
	See "Reading and Understanding Information Displayed in Tables" on page 87.
	You will need to mention the airport's name and your name when you answer the call.
	See "Using the Telephone and Making Telephone Calls" on page 104.

Interpreting Tables and Taking a Telephone Call

Scenario

You work in the "Flight Enquiries" Department of Isaac Newton Airport and part of your job is to provide flight information to callers.

Activities

Your tutor will take the part of a person enquiring about flights to Paris.

1   Have in front of you the **Flight Timetable to Paris document (Appendix 1)**. Listen to what the caller has to say and give him/her the information he/she needs.

2   The caller will not ask the check-in details so you must be prepared to give the caller this information.

3   Finish the call by asking if there is any further help you can give.

ISAAC NEWTON AIRPORT
FLIGHT TIMETABLE TO PARIS
Service Dates : 31 March to 30 October
ISAAC NEWTON TO PARIS (CDG)*

Flight Days**	Departing	Flight No	Flight Length	Airline
1,4,5,6,7	0730	WS556	1 hour 10 mins	Wings Air
2,5,6	0745	PA2877	1 hour	Paris Air
1,2,3,4,5,6,7	0900	EF378	1 hour 10 mins	EasyFly
2,4,6	1130	WS559	1 hour 10 mins	Wings Air
3,5,7	1350	CA777	1 hour 15 mins	Channel Air
2,3,5,7	1950	EF228	1 hour 10 mins	EasyFly
2,4,5	2020	PA2851	1 hour	Paris Air

PARIS (CDG) TO ISAAC NEWTON

Flight Days**	Departing	Flight No	Flight Length	Airline
2,5,6	0700	CA707	1 hour 15 mins	Channel Air
3,5,6,7	0915	PA2651	1 hour	Paris Air
1,2,3,4,5,6	1050	WS523	1 hour 10 mins	Wings Air
1,4,5	1300	CA721	1 hour 15 mins	Channel Air
2,3,6,7	1450	EF227	1 hour 10 mins	EasyFly
2,3,5,7	1600	PA2850	1 hour	Paris Air
1,4,5	1935	EF221	1 hour 10 mins	EasyFly

* Charles de Gaulle Airport

** 1 = Monday; 2 = Tuesday; 3 = Wednesday; 4 = Thursday; 5 = Friday;
6 = Saturday; 7 = Sunday

Check in time at both airports is 2 hours before flight time

Solutions to Exercises for Section 1

Page 6

1 We're
2 It's
3 They're
4 isn't
5 I'm
6 It's   haven't
7 What's
8 It's   they're
9 You're   aren't
10 it'll   I've

Page 10

1 the boy's hat
2 the chair's legs
3 the man's briefcase
4 the dog's bone
5 the student's pen

Page 13

1 the clubs' football ground
2 the students' text books
3 the tutors' pens
4 the cars' exhausts
5 the boxers' competitions

Page 14

1 The cat's toy
2 The school's trophy
3 The piano's keys
4 The cats' whiskers
5 The gentlemen's club
6 The policemen's uniforms
7 The student's book
8 The woman's umbrella
9 The car's steering wheel
10 The man's briefcase

Page 15

1 achieve
2 believe
3 ceiling
4 freight
5 neighbours
6 piece
7 priest
8 receipt
9 reign
10 relief
11 sleigh
12 veins
13 weigh
14 yield

Page 16

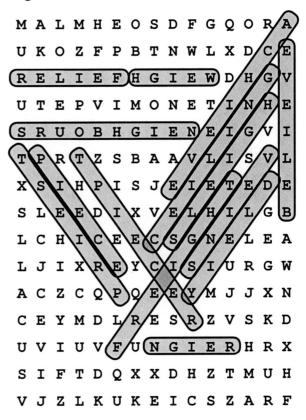

Page 18

1 their
2 there
3 there
4 there
5 They're   their   there
6 they're
7 They're
8 Their
9 There   their
10 They're   their

Page 21

1 to
2 too to
3 two to
4 to two too
5 to two
6 too
7 to
8 too   to too

Page 23

1 Where
2 Were
3 Where
4 we're
5 where
6 Were   where   were
7 we're
8 where
9 We're we're
10 Where

Page 25

1 hear
2 here
3 here
4 hear

5 heard here
6 heard
7 here heard
8 hear   here
9 here
10 here   heard

Page 27

1 number
2 number
3 amount
4 number
5 amount
6 number
7 amount
8 amount
9 number
10 amount

Page 29

1 less
2 fewer
3 fewer
4 less
5 less
6 fewer
7 fewer
8 less
9 fewer
10 fewer

Page 31

1 advice
2 advice
3 advise
4 advice
5 advise
6 advise
7 advice

8   advise
9   advice
10 advise

Page 33
1   practise
2   practise
3   practice
4   practice
5   practise
6   practise
7   practise
8   practice
9   practise
10 practice

Page 35
1   right
2   write
3   right
4   write
5   right
6   write
7   Right
8   right   write
9   write   right
10 write

Page 37
1   took
2   taken
3   took
4   took
5   taken
6   taken
7   taken
8   taken
9   taken
10 taken

Page 39
1   incorrect
2   correct
3   incorrect
4   correct
5   incorrect
6   incorrect
7   incorrect
8   correct
9   correct
10 incorrect

Page 41
1   loose
2   loose
3   lose
4   lose
5   loose
6   lose
7   loose
8   lose
9   lose
10 loose

Page 43
1   borrow
2   lent
3   borrow
4   lend
5   lend
6   borrow
7   lend
8   borrowed
9   lend
10 borrow

Page 45
1   learn
2   teach

3   learn

4   teach

5   teach

6   teach

7   learn

8   teach

9   learn

10 taught   learn

Page 47

1   went

2   gone

3   gone

4   went

5   gone

6   went

7   gone

8   gone

9   gone   went

10 gone

Page 49

1   have

2   have

3   have

4   of

5   of

6   have

7   of

8   have

9   have

10 have

Page 51

1   correct

2   incorrect

3   correct

4   correct

5   correct

6   correct

7   correct

8   incorrect

Page 54

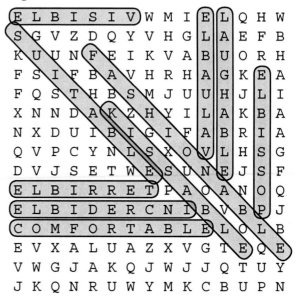

Page 59

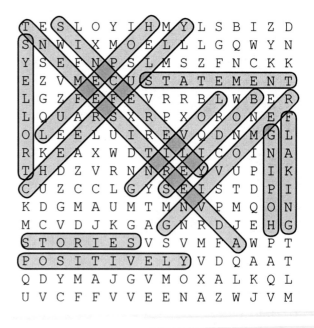